The Little Encyclopedia of the Human Body

The Little Encyclopedia of the Human Body

Richard Walker

KINGFISHER

NEW YORK

Editors Julie Ferris, Jonathan Stroud

Designer Malcolm Parchment

Consultant Dr. Roy Palmer

Photography Geoff Dann, Tim Ridley

Illustrations Alan Hancocks, Guy Smith,
Gina Suter

Picture Research Manager Jane Lambert

DTP Coordinator Nicky Studdart

Production Controller Richard Waterhouse

Artwork Archivist Steve Robinson

Index Sue Lightfoot

KINGFISHER
80 Maiden Lane
New York, New York 10038
www.kingfisherpub.com

First published as *First Encyclopedia of the Human Body*
by Kingfisher Publications Plc 1999
Reprinted in a revised format in 2001

2 4 6 8 10 9 7 5 3 1
ITR/0701/SF/SOT(MAR)/150MA

LIBRARY OF CONGRESS CATALOGING-IN-PUBLICATION DATA
has been applied for.

ISBN 0-7534-5423-8

Printed in China

Your book

Your *Little Encyclopedia of the Human Body* is the perfect way of finding out all about the human body. Packed with exciting information, amazing facts, and colorful pictures, it can be used for school projects or just for fun.

△ The information about each picture is printed next to it. The arrows show you which information goes with which picture.

this muscle straightens the fingers

a band of fibers holds the tendons in place

▷ Labels on some pictures give extra information. Follow the lines to find out what the different parts do.

tendon from the muscle that straightens the fingers

Kidney sieve

Mix together some salt and sugar and shake it in a sieve over a bowl. The salt passes through the sieve while the sugar stays in it. Your kidneys sift blood so that you lose waste, but keep nutrients.

Find Out More

If you want to find out more about any topic, look at this box. It will tell you which pages to look at.

△ Instructions and photographs in the colored boxes show you how to do the activities.

Contents

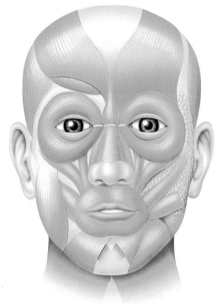

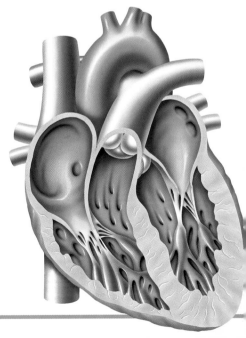

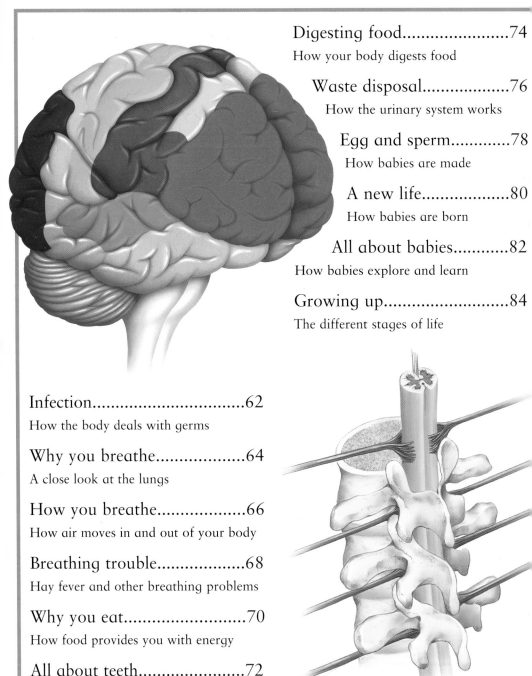

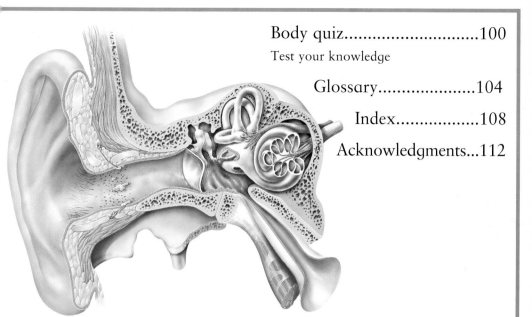

Our bodies

Sit quietly for a moment. Listen to yourself breathing. Put your hand in the middle of your chest and feel your heart beating. Think about what you most like to do. Now consider the fact that these body activities—breathing, the beating of your heart, and thinking— are being experienced at the same time by six billion people around the world.

△ Variety is the spice of life! Look at this group of boys and girls and you can see different heights, different skin colors, different faces, and different hair. However, although we all look very different from each other, we all share the fact that we belong to the human family.

△ Humans are divided into two main groups—females and males. The differences between them become more obvious when they are grown up. Women have more rounded bodies with broader hips, while men usually have more muscular bodies with broader shoulders.

△ Everyone needs to eat. Food provides you with the energy your body needs to keep it running normally. It also gives you building material that enables you to grow.

△ Two thirds of your body is made up of water. You need to drink to replace the water you lose when you sweat or go to the bathroom.

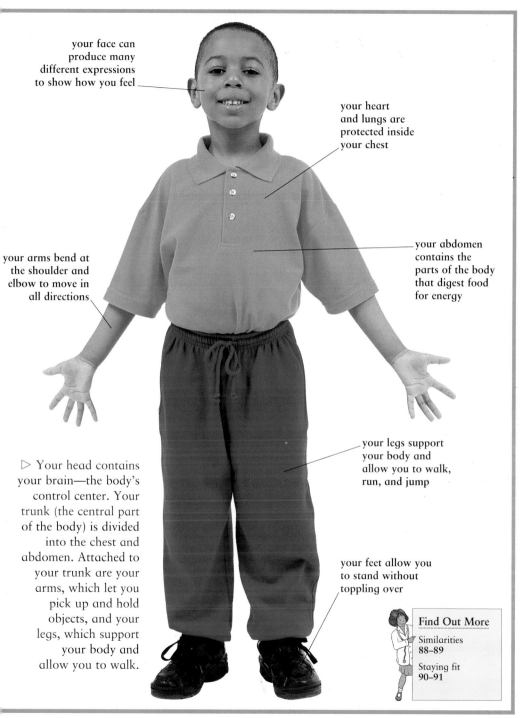

your face can produce many different expressions to show how you feel

your heart and lungs are protected inside your chest

your arms bend at the shoulder and elbow to move in all directions

your abdomen contains the parts of the body that digest food for energy

▷ Your head contains your brain—the body's control center. Your trunk (the central part of the body) is divided into the chest and abdomen. Attached to your trunk are your arms, which let you pick up and hold objects, and your legs, which support your body and allow you to walk.

your legs support your body and allow you to walk, run, and jump

your feet allow you to stand without toppling over

Find Out More

Similarities
88–89

Staying fit
90–91

Cells

Your body is made up of millions and millions of microscopic cells. Each cell is a tiny, living unit with a complex inner structure. There are many different types of cells in the body, each with its own shape, size, and job to do. Cells of the same type are grouped together as tissue.

△ Every sperm cell has a head and a tail. Sperm swim along by moving their tails from side to side.

▷ A muscle cell is sometimes called a muscle fiber. To make your body move, the long, striped muscle fibers contract (get shorter) and pull on your bones.

◁ Your liver is packed with cube-shaped cells. Blood flows along the spaces between them. As it does, liver cells busily clean the blood and make sure it contains the correct ingredients.

membrane surrounds the cell

▷ Looking like doughnut-shaped cushions, red blood cells carry life-giving oxygen to where it is needed. The blood cells tumble over each other as blood surges along an artery (a tube that carries blood around the body).

jellylike cytoplasm contains organelles

▽ Cells may appear different from the outside, but inside they have a lot in common. Each cell has a nucleus (center) that controls what it does. It also has many different organelles ("tiny organs") that keep the cell working properly.

▷ This liver cell is one of many different kinds of cells inside the body.

these channels move substances around the cell

mitochondria are organelles that supply energy

▷ Liver cells of the same type are grouped together to form tissue.

ribosomes are organelles that make cell-building proteins

▷ Together, different tissues form an organ, in this case the liver.

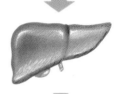

nucleus (center) of the cell

▷ The liver and other organs form the digestive system.

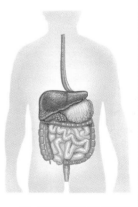

▷ Inside your brain there are billions of nerve cells. Each has branches that connect it to other nerve cells. Messages flash along these branches so that you can think and feel.

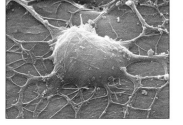

Find Out More

Hormones
54–55

Egg and sperm
78–79

Outer covering

Your skin covers your body like a living overcoat. Although it is only $\frac{1}{10}$ inch thick, skin forms a barrier between you and the outside world. It keep germs from getting inside your body, protects you from damage and the harmful rays in sunlight, and keeps you from drying out.

hair

◁ A closer look at the skin reveals a crisscross pattern of lines. The hairs grow from holes called follicles.

epidermis {

▷ Under a microscope, the surface of the skin looks scaly and flaky. Every year, nine pounds of flakes are worn away from your skin.

dermis

sweat gland

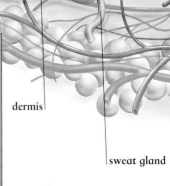

Looking at skin

To see what your skin really looks like, use a magnifying glass. Hold it above your arm and then move it slowly until the skin's surface comes into focus. What can you see? Is your skin smooth, or are there lines and wrinkles? Can you see any skin flakes? Now look at the skin on your fingertips. Can you see any patterns? Are there any hairs?

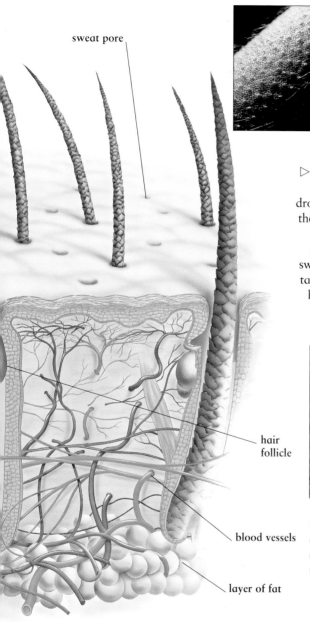

sweat pore

hair follicle

blood vessels

layer of fat

◁ If you get cold or scared, goosebumps like these appear on your skin. This happens because tiny muscles in the skin tug at the hair follicles, making the hairs stand upright, and the skin bumpy.

▷ This microscopic picture shows droplets of sweat on the skin of someone who is hot from exercising. As the sweat evaporates, it takes heat from the body and helps to cool it down.

△ Tiny parasitic creatures sometimes live on human skin. Skin mites feed on skin flakes. Itch mites, like the one pictured here, burrow into the skin to lay eggs.

Find Out More

Skin deep
16–17

Touch
50–51

△ Skin has two layers—the epidermis and the dermis. The epidermis forms a protective covering. Its cells are constantly worn away and replaced. The dermis contains sweat glands and blood vessels. A layer of fat under the dermis helps keep you warm.

Skin deep

The color of your skin is produced in the thin, outer epidermis. It contains melanin, a brown pigment (coloring) that helps protect the dermis from the harmful effects of sunlight. When exposed to sunlight, your skin naturally makes extra melanin to darken your skin and provide extra protection.

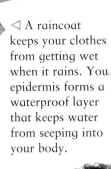

◁ A raincoat keeps your clothes from getting wet when it rains. You epidermis forms a waterproof layer that keeps water from seeping into your body.

◁ Normally the temperature inside your body stays the same. A layer of fat under the skin helps keep you warm. Unless the weather is very hot, you also need to wear clothes to keep the heat in.

▷ Sunlight can burn your skin or, in some cases, cause a serious disease called skin cancer. Suntan lotions and sunblocks rubbed on the skin, as well as hats and loose clothes, all help stop sunlight from damaging your skin.

▽ These babies show the wide variety of skin colors found in human beings. Human skin colors range through thousands of shades, from pale pink to very dark brown. Skin color depends on how much melanin is made in the epidermis. The more melanin there is, the darker a person's skin. Pale skin is given a pinkish color by the blood flowing just below its surface.

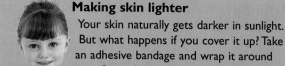

Making skin lighter

Your skin naturally gets darker in sunlight. But what happens if you cover it up? Take an adhesive bandage and wrap it around one finger. Leave it in place for a few days and then remove it. You will find that the skin covered by the bandage has gotten lighter in color. The plaster stops sunlight from reaching the skin, so it makes less melanin.

△ This girl has freckles on her face. These are tiny patches of skin that contain more than the usual amount of melanin. Freckles are more easily seen on people with lighter skin.

▷ If you hit or knock your skin, some of the tiny blood vessels in it may break and leak. You can see this leakage of blood as a bruise. Bruises are normally blue or black at first, then turn yellow. A bruise near the eye is usually called a "black eye."

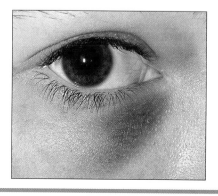

Find Out More

Outer covering
14–15

Hands
30–31

All about hair

Although millions of hairs cover your body, they are mostly too short and fine to keep you warm. Only the long hairs on your head keep heat in. Hair grows from pits in the skin called follicles. Head hairs grow about $\frac{1}{10}$ inch a week for a few years, then stop growing. The hairs fall out and are replaced by new ones.

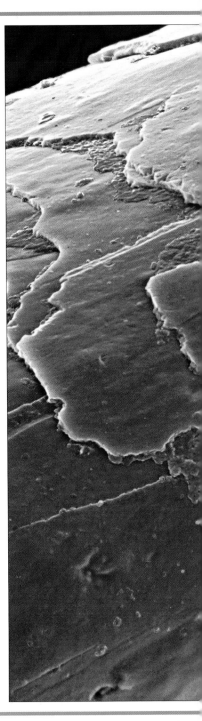

◁ Some men are bald because their head hairs grow for only a short time. The hairs do not grow long enough to stick out from the follicles before falling out.

▷ Long, thick hair grows on men's faces. Many men shave daily to remove this hair. Others let it grow into a mustache and beard.

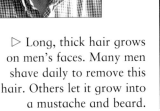

Hairy sensors

Carefully run your fingers over the hairs on your arms without touching the surface of your skin. You should feel a sensation of very light touch even though your finger does not make contact with your skin. As you touch the hairs you move the touch sensors at their base. The sensors send signals to the brain so that you can feel even the gentlest touch.

△ Hair color ranges from blonde to black depending on the amount of melanin, the brown pigment that also colors skin. Hair can be straight, wavy, or curly, depending on the shape of the follicles from which the hair grows.

▷ Straight hairs grow from hair follicles that are rounded in shape.

▷ Wavy hairs grow from hair follicles that are oval in shape.

▷ Curly hairs grow from hair follicles that are flattened in shape.

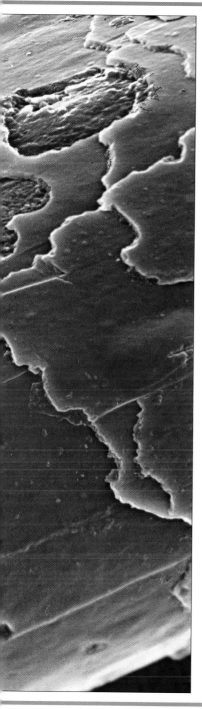

◁ This is a highly magnified view of a hair. The outside of the hair is covered by plates that overlap like fish scales. They stop hairs from sticking together. Hair cells are dead. This is why it does not hurt when you have your hair cut.

Find Out More

Our bodies
10–11

Outer covering
14–15

Bony frame

Your body is supported by a bony frame called the skeleton. This is made of 206 bones that link together to form a strong but flexible framework. The skeleton protects important organs, such as the brain and heart, and anchors the muscles that allow you to move. Before birth, the skeleton is made of a softer material called cartilage.

△ Tent poles support a tent and give it shape. Without them, the tent collapses and is shapeless. Your skeleton does exactly the same job for your body. Without your bones, your body would immediately collapse into a floppy mess.

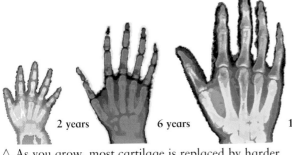

2 years   6 years   19 years

△ As you grow, most cartilage is replaced by harder bone. In these X rays, bone shows up but cartilage does not. In a two-year-old's hand, there are big gaps between bones where cartilage is present. By the age of six, bone is replacing cartilage. In an adult hand, the bones are fully formed, and there is little cartilage.

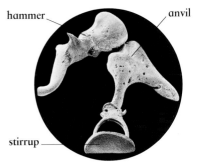

hammer   anvil

stirrup

Feel your cartilage

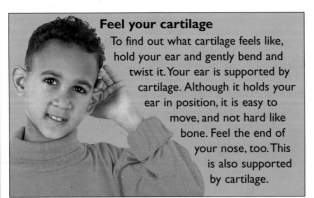

To find out what cartilage feels like, hold your ear and gently bend and twist it. Your ear is supported by cartilage. Although it holds your ear in position, it is easy to move, and not hard like bone. Feel the end of your nose, too. This is also supported by cartilage.

△ Your smallest bones are the three tiny ossicles in your ear. They are also called the hammer, anvil, and stirrup because of their shapes. They help carry sounds into your ear, so you can hear. The tiniest one, the stirrup, is just $1/8$ inch long.

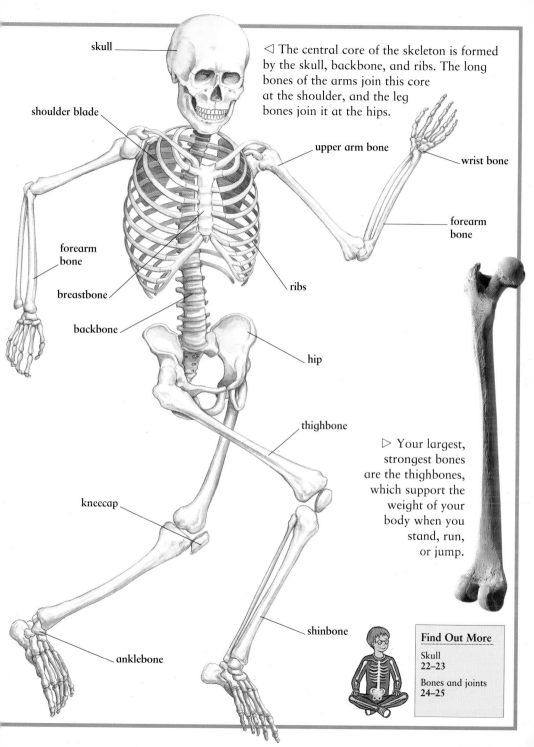

skull

shoulder blade

upper arm bone

wrist bone

◁ The central core of the skeleton is formed by the skull, backbone, and ribs. The long bones of the arms join this core at the shoulder, and the leg bones join it at the hips.

forearm bone

forearm bone

breastbone

ribs

backbone

hip

thighbone

kneecap

▷ Your largest, strongest bones are the thighbones, which support the weight of your body when you stand, run, or jump.

shinbone

anklebone

Find Out More

Skull
22–23

Bones and joints
24–25

Skull

Your bony skull gives shape to your head and face. It surrounds the soft, delicate brain and keeps it from being crushed or damaged. Openings in the skull form entrances to the ears, nose, and mouth. The eye sockets act like protective pockets, allowing the eyes to swivel. Rows of strong teeth are firmly anchored in the jawbone, ready to bite and chew food.

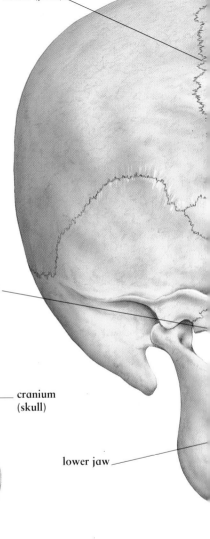

suture (joint)

cheekbone

cranium (skull)

lower jaw

brain

eyeball in socket

◁ This "exploded" skull shows how the bones that form it are perfectly shaped to fit together. Where the bones meet they have jagged edges that lock tightly into each other like the pieces of a jigsaw puzzle. This makes the skull very strong.

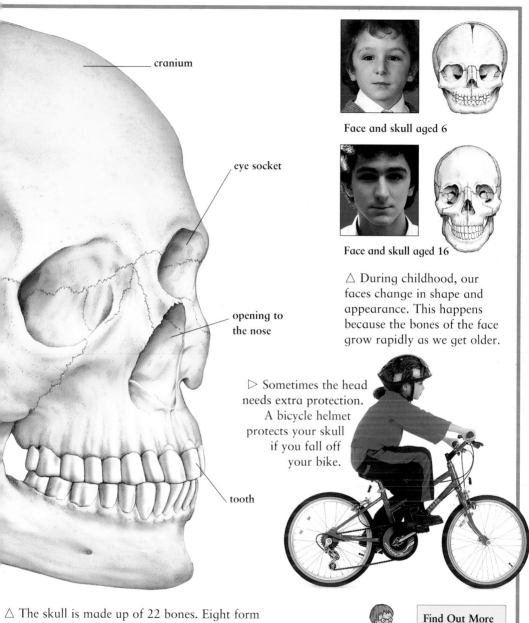

cranium

eye socket

opening to
the nose

tooth

Face and skull aged 6

Face and skull aged 16

△ During childhood, our
faces change in shape and
appearance. This happens
because the bones of the face
grow rapidly as we get older.

▷ Sometimes the head
needs extra protection.
A bicycle helmet
protects your skull
if you fall off
your bike.

△ The skull is made up of 22 bones. Eight form
the cranium, the bony box that surrounds the brain.
The other 14 bones make up the face. Nearly all the
bones are firmly locked together by unmoving joints
called sutures. Only the lower jaw is able to move
freely, allowing you to eat and speak.

Find Out More

Bones and joints
24–25

Control center
34–35

Bones and joints

Bones are living organs with their own cells and blood supply. They are formed from materials that make them both hard and strong. In the skeleton, bones meet at joints. Most joints are movable, which allows the skeleton to change position. Different joints allow different kinds of movement.

▽ Bones have an outer layer of compact bone that is very hard. It surrounds a layer of lighter spongy bone. The hollow middle of the bone is filled with jellylike bone marrow. This structure makes living bones five times stronger than steel.

a membrane protects the bone

spongy bone

compact bone

◁ Hinge joints work like a door hinge. They allow bones to move up and down, but not from side to side. You can see a hinge joint in action when you bend or straighten your knee.

Hinge joint

▷ Ball-and-socket joints allow movement in many directions. The rounded end of one bone fits inside the cup-shaped socket of another bone. In the shoulder, the end of the arm bone fits into a socket formed by the shoulder bones.

Ball-and-socket joint

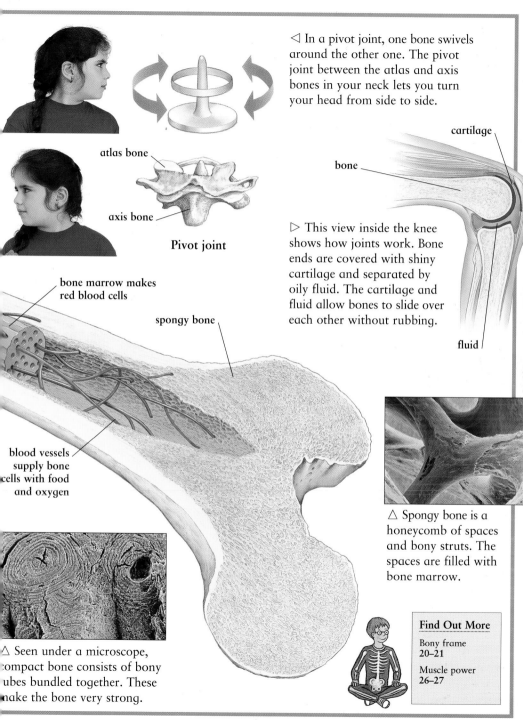

◁ In a pivot joint, one bone swivels around the other one. The pivot joint between the atlas and axis bones in your neck lets you turn your head from side to side.

cartilage

atlas bone

bone

axis bone

Pivot joint

▷ This view inside the knee shows how joints work. Bone ends are covered with shiny cartilage and separated by oily fluid. The cartilage and fluid allow bones to slide over each other without rubbing.

fluid

bone marrow makes red blood cells

spongy bone

blood vessels supply bone cells with food and oxygen

△ Spongy bone is a honeycomb of spaces and bony struts. The spaces are filled with bone marrow.

△ Seen under a microscope, compact bone consists of bony tubes bundled together. These make the bone very strong.

Find Out More

Bony frame
20–21

Muscle power
26–27

Muscle power

Every movement that you make uses muscles. Without them, you could not run, walk, smile, or speak. Muscles can contract when told to do so by the brain. Each muscle is attached to two or more bones by tough cords called tendons. When the muscle contracts, it pulls on the bones and makes the body move.

▷ Every time you move, your brain has to control many muscles at once. Some activities, like running, need hundreds of muscles working together at the same time. To move with the skill and grace of a dancer you need strong muscles and plenty of practice.

▷ The muscles that move the body lie just under the skin. Besides producing movement, they give the body its shape. Here, you can see some of a dancer's main muscles and what they do. You have the same muscles in your body.

running

turning somersaults

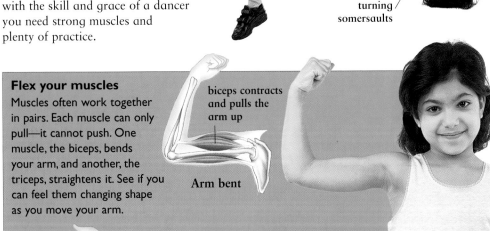

Flex your muscles

Muscles often work together in pairs. Each muscle can only pull—it cannot push. One muscle, the biceps, bends your arm, and another, the triceps, straightens it. See if you can feel them changing shape as you move your arm.

biceps contracts and pulls the arm up

Arm bent

biceps relaxes

muscle attached to bone by tendon

Arm straight

triceps contracts and pulls the arm down

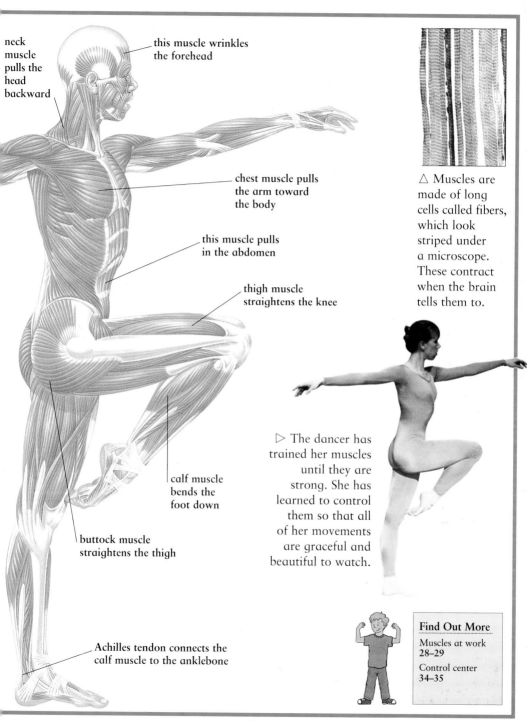

neck muscle pulls the head backward

this muscle wrinkles the forehead

chest muscle pulls the arm toward the body

this muscle pulls in the abdomen

thigh muscle straightens the knee

△ Muscles are made of long cells called fibers, which look striped under a microscope. These contract when the brain tells them to.

calf muscle bends the foot down

buttock muscle straightens the thigh

▷ The dancer has trained her muscles until they are strong. She has learned to control them so that all of her movements are graceful and beautiful to watch.

Achilles tendon connects the calf muscle to the anklebone

Find Out More

Muscles at work
28–29

Control center
34–35

Muscles at work

There are over 640 skeletal muscles in your body. They produce a wide range of movements, depending on their size and strength, and on the bones and joints with which they work. Muscles in the face and neck make facial expressions. Other muscles support your body when you are awake. As muscles work, they release heat. This helps keep your body warm.

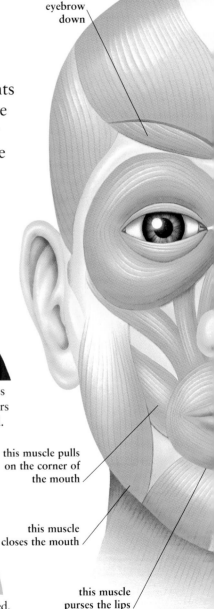

this muscle pulls the eyebrow down

this muscle pulls on the corner of the mouth

this muscle closes the mouth

this muscle purses the lips

△ When you frown, muscles pull your eyebrows down and toward each other.

△ If you feel sad, muscles in your chin pull the corners of your mouth downward.

△ To smile, muscles in your cheeks pull the corners of your mouth upward.

△ When you look surprised, muscles raise your eyebrows and open your eyes wide.

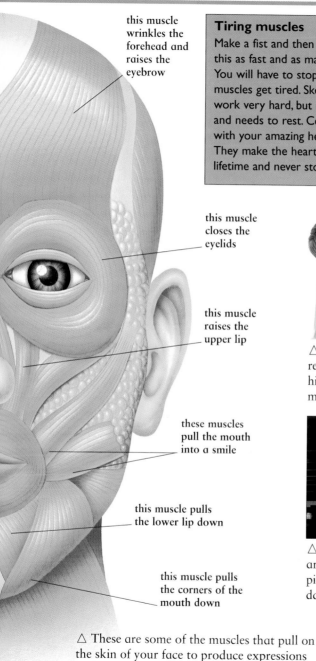

this muscle wrinkles the forehead and raises the eyebrow

this muscle closes the eyelids

this muscle raises the upper lip

△ This sleeping boy's muscles have relaxed and provide less support for his body. The girl is awake and her muscles keep her upright.

these muscles pull the mouth into a smile

this muscle pulls the lower lip down

△ After exercise, this man's muscles are hot and look white in a heat picture. As they cool, they get darker.

this muscle pulls the corners of the mouth down

△ These are some of the muscles that pull on the skin of your face to produce expressions such as smiling or frowning. These expressions communicate your feelings to other people.

Find Out More

Communication
52–53

Inside the heart
56–57

Hands

Each of your hands contains 27 bones, making them the most flexible parts of your body. Unlike most other animals, humans walk upright, so their hands are free to be used as tools. Over 30 muscles in the forearm and hands move your wrists, palms, thumbs, and fingers. This allows you to perform all kinds of tasks.

▽ Most of the muscles that move your fingers are found not in the hand, but in the arm. They are attached to the hand and finger bones by very long tendons. You can see your own tendons move by looking at the back of your hand and bending your fingers.

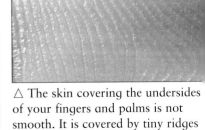

this muscle straightens the fingers

this muscle straightens the wrist

a band of fibers holds the tendons in place

△ Some people—and you may be one of them—have difficulty using their hands. This does not keep them from drawing or writing, however. This woman is using a special tool attached to her head to help her draw.

Tied fingers

Write your name on a piece of paper. Now take a rubber band and wrap it around your fingers so that they cannot move. Try to write your name again. It is very difficult. Your fingers must be free to form the special grip that you use to write.

△ The skin covering the undersides of your fingers and palms is not smooth. It is covered by tiny ridges that help you grip things.

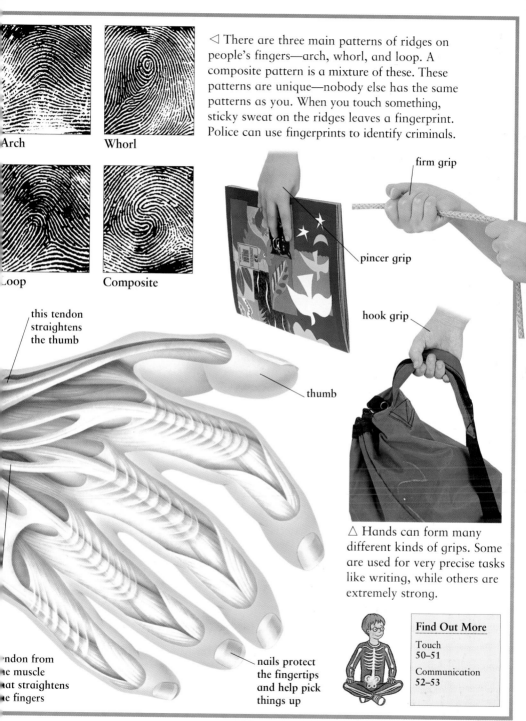

Arch

Whorl

Loop

Composite

◁ There are three main patterns of ridges on people's fingers—arch, whorl, and loop. A composite pattern is a mixture of these. These patterns are unique—nobody else has the same patterns as you. When you touch something, sticky sweat on the ridges leaves a fingerprint. Police can use fingerprints to identify criminals.

firm grip

pincer grip

hook grip

this tendon straightens the thumb

thumb

△ Hands can form many different kinds of grips. Some are used for very precise tasks like writing, while others are extremely strong.

tendon from the muscle that straightens the fingers

nails protect the fingertips and help pick things up

Find Out More

Touch
50–51

Communication
52–53

Nervous network

The nervous system is a massive communication network that controls how the body works. It lets you feel, move, and think, and it controls all the inner workings of your body without you even noticing. Your nervous system is made up of billions of nerve cells called neurons. These long, thin cells carry electrical messages at high speed all around your body.

nerve

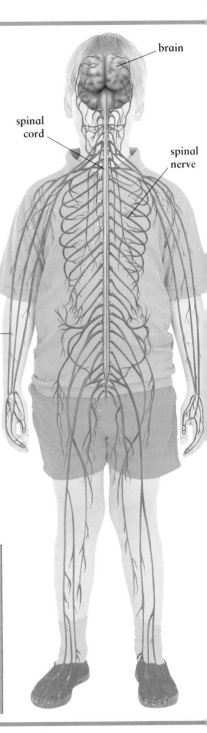

brain

spinal cord

spinal nerve

▷ Your brain is the control center of your nervous system. It receives information from your body, sorts and stores it, and sends out messages telling your body what to do. Information is carried to and from all parts of the body along a network of long nerves. The spinal cord is the most important route in the network. Many pairs of spinal nerves branch out from it.

Reaction times

Find out how quickly your nervous system works. Hold your hand in front of you like the girl on the left. Tell your friend to let a ruler drop between your fingers. As soon as you see it falling, try to catch it. The closer you are to clasping the bottom of the ruler, the faster your reaction time has been.

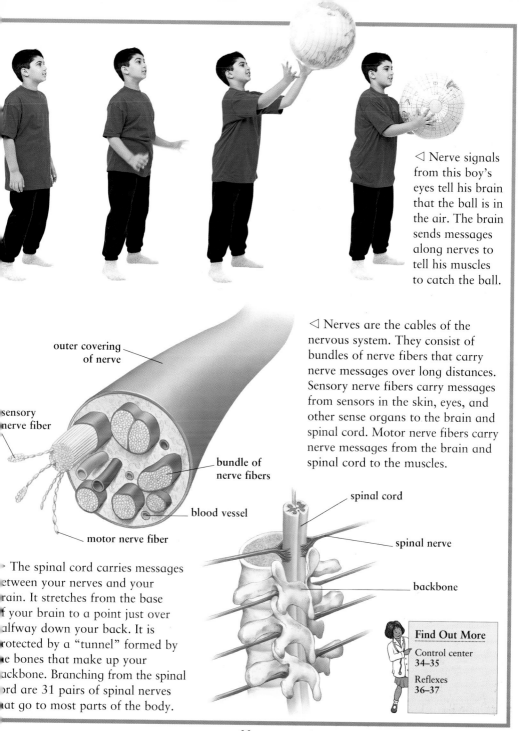

◁ Nerve signals from this boy's eyes tell his brain that the ball is in the air. The brain sends messages along nerves to tell his muscles to catch the ball.

outer covering of nerve

sensory nerve fiber

bundle of nerve fibers

blood vessel

motor nerve fiber

◁ Nerves are the cables of the nervous system. They consist of bundles of nerve fibers that carry nerve messages over long distances. Sensory nerve fibers carry messages from sensors in the skin, eyes, and other sense organs to the brain and spinal cord. Motor nerve fibers carry nerve messages from the brain and spinal cord to the muscles.

spinal cord

spinal nerve

backbone

▷ The spinal cord carries messages between your nerves and your brain. It stretches from the base of your brain to a point just over halfway down your back. It is protected by a "tunnel" formed by the bones that make up your backbone. Branching from the spinal cord are 31 pairs of spinal nerves that go to most parts of the body.

Find Out More

Control center
34–35

Reflexes
36–37

Control center

Your body's control center is the brain. It lets you think, feel, move, remember, and be happy or sad. It also controls all the other parts of the body. The thinking, feeling part of the brain is called the cerebrum. Its left half controls the right side of your body, and its right half controls the left.

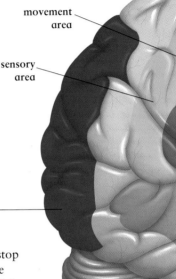

◁ The brain's movement area sends messages to your muscles, telling them to contract so that your body moves

movement area

sensory area

vision area

▷ Millions of touch sensors in your skin send messages to your brain's sensory area. They help you feel whether things are hard or soft.

◁ Your eyes send a nonstop stream of messages to the vision area at the back of the brain. This turns the messages into pictures that you can see.

Use your brain

Look at this picture of the brain—it is the same as the bigger one in the middle of the page—and try to answer this quiz. Which part of the brain are you using when you a) look at this page, b) turn a page, c) touch the picture, d) figure out the answers to these questions?

Answers: a) 1; b) 3; c) 2; d) 6

△ Hearing areas receive nerve messages from your ears and turn them into sounds you can hear.

▽ This shows the right half of the cerebrum. Each area has its own job. Some receive messages from sensors in the body, and some send out messages to muscles. Other areas let you think and understand.

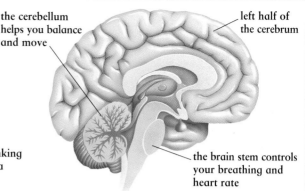

the cerebellum helps you balance and move

left half of the cerebrum

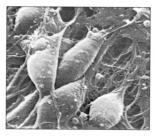

thinking area

speech area (usually found on the left side of the brain)

hearing area

the brain stem controls your breathing and heart rate

△ This section through the middle of the brain shows its three main parts: the cerebrum, the cerebellum and the brain stem. They all play different roles.

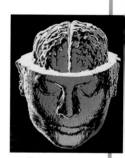

▷ This special 3-D X ray shows the head of a living person. It allows a doctor to "remove" the top of the skull to see the surface of the patient's brain.

◁ This image shows a few of the 100 billion neurons found in your cerebrum. They all connect to make a communication network more complex than any computer.

◁ Are you right- or left-handed? It depends on which half of your brain is in charge. Writing with the "wrong" hand is harder because it uses the brain's other half.

Find Out More

Learning
38–39

Sleep
40–41

Reflexes

Reflexes are automatic, superfast actions performed by the body in response to a sensation. They are controlled by nerve messages that work without you even thinking about them. Some reflexes protect your body from danger, such as the one that automatically pulls your hand away from a sharp object.

spinal cord

1. The finger is pricked by sharp spines on the cactus.

2. Sensory neurons carry a nerve message to the spinal cord.

Test a friend's reflexes

Ask a friend to stand in front of you. Without warning, clap your hand in front of their face. Your friend will blink. This is a reflex that protects the sensitive eyes from anything that might be about to hit them. If you had to think about blinking, your eyes could easily be hurt before you could close them.

△ While touching a cactus, this girl pricks her finger on a sharp spine. Sensors in her finger instantly send a message along sensory neurons to her spinal cord. The spinal cord then sends messages along motor neurons to her arm muscle telling it to move her finger. All this happens in a split second. Only then does the message reach her brain. She feels the pain and cries "Ouch!"

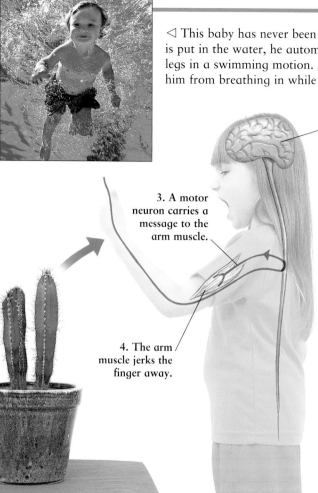

◁ This baby has never been swimming before, but when he is put in the water, he automatically moves his arms and legs in a swimming motion. Another reflex action keeps him from breathing in while his head is under water.

5. The nerve message arrives in the brain and the girl feels pain.

3. A motor neuron carries a message to the arm muscle.

4. The arm muscle jerks the finger away.

△ Babies are born with a set of simple, built-in reflexes. One of these is the walking reflex. When the doctor holds the baby with her feet touching the ground, she makes walking movements. These reflexes disappear after a few months.

◁ Doctors use reflexes to test whether the nervous system is working well. Here, a doctor gently taps the boy's knee with a hammer. When he does this, the boy's lower leg should move. This shows that nerve messages are passing normally between the knee, the spinal cord, and the muscles in the leg.

Find Out More

Nervous network
32–33

All about babies
82–83

Learning

From birth to the late teens, humans learn the skills they need in life. Learning depends on memory—the ability the brain has to store and recall information. Movement skills, such as walking, are learned by trial and error. Languages and facts and figures are learned by listening and reading.

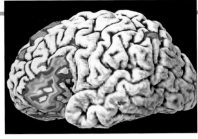

△ To speak you need to learn words. This picture shows the area in the brain that is active when you speak.

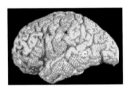
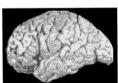

◁ Seeing and listening play an important part in learning. These scans show the brain at work taking in new information. In the top scan, the person is looking at words in a book. In the bottom scan, she is hearing words being spoken.

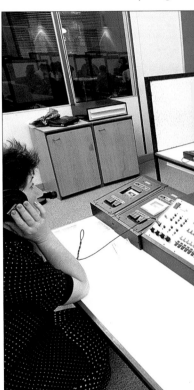

△ In a language lab, a class listens to their teacher as they learn a foreign language. To learn a new language, you have to listen to it or read it, and then store the words away in your memory. The more you practice, the easier it becomes to remember the words.

△ Playing chess requires a lot of skills. First, you have to learn the moves that each chess piece can make. As you get more experienced, you start to learn how to combine these moves on the board. Only then are you able plan several moves in advance in order to beat your opponent.

◁ By holding on to a chair, this baby is able to pull herself upright. Once she gets used to standing up, she will take her first steps. She will slowly learn to walk by trial and error. If she moves and does not fall over, the experience will be stored in her memory.

△ This girl uses a cart for extra support as she walks. As she learns to walk in a more controlled way, her movements become less jerky. Every time she tries, she improves a little.

△ At the age of one, this girl can stand up and take a few steps without any support. But she still loses her balance from time to time and falls down.

◁ Cycling is another skill that has to be learned. This child can pedal with her feet to move the bicycle forward, and she can steer with her hands. She is not able to balance yet without training wheels for support.

Find Out More

Control center
34–35

Growing up
84–85

Sleep

Sleep is essential for health. It allows your body to rest, and your brain to sort the information it received that day. People who don't get enough sleep soon get sick. Every night, you have periods of deep sleep, when your brain is not very active. During lighter sleep, when your brain is active, your eyes move under your eyelids and you dream.

◁ In the evening, your brain activity changes as it gets ready for sleep. You want to lie down because you are too tired to stand or sit, and your eyelids feel heavy and start to close. Now you are ready for bed

△ The number of hours you need to sleep each night goes down as you get older. Babies sleep for 16 hours each day, but a five-year-old child needs only about 12 hours' sleep. Adults need about eight hours' sleep.

Keep a dream diary

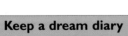

When you wake up each morning, write down the details of any dreams you can remember. You will probably find that your dreams mix up many events, facts, and people. This is because dreams happen while the brain is sorting out all the messages it receives during the day and compares them with information already stored in the memory.

△ You usually wake up in a different position from the one you went to sleep in. This is because you move during deep sleep. During lighter sleep, your muscles are paralyzed so you don't act out your dreams!

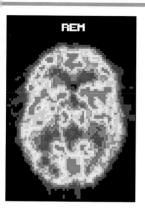
REM

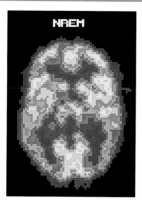
NREM

◁ These pictures are produced by a machine called a PET scanner. This scans a person's brain to see which parts of it are active. Active areas are red, and inactive areas are blue. The left scan shows a person in light, dreaming sleep. The right scan shows a person in deep sleep. You can see that the brain is more active in light sleep than deep sleep.

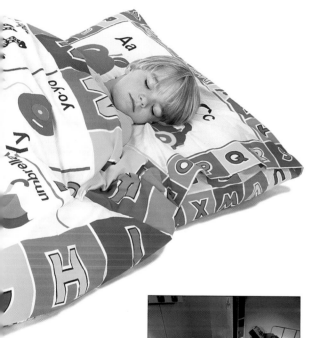

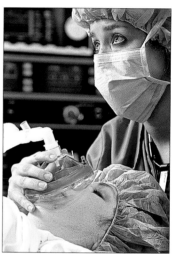

△ This patient is about to have an operation. A doctor is giving her an anesthetic to keep her unconscious during the operation. She will feel no pain and cannot wake up as she could if she was asleep.

▷ Your brain produces electrical signals called brain waves. These change as you go from deep to light sleep. Here, the pattern of a sleeper's brain waves are being recorded by a machine.

Find Out More

Control center
34–35

Learning
38–39

How you see

Your eyes allow you to see your surroundings. When light from the thing you are looking at hits sensors in your eyes, they send messages to the brain. Your brain sorts out the messages and forms pictures that you can "see." Only a small part of the eye can be seen because each eyeball is protected within a bony socket in the skull.

△ At the center of the iris (the colored part of the eye) is a hole called the pupil, which lets light enter the eye.

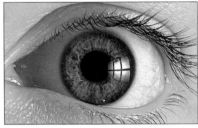

△ In bright light, the iris makes the pupil smaller. This reduces the amount of light going into the eye. In dim light, the pupil is wider.

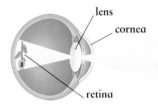

lens
cornea
retina

△ When you look at something, light from that object enters your eye. Light passes through the clear cornea at the front of your eye, and then through the transparent lens. The cornea and lens focus the light so that it forms a clear, upside-down image on the retina at the back of your eye. Sensors in the retina detect the image and send nerve messages along the optic nerve to your brain where the image is "seen" right-side up.

Blind spot test

Hold this book in front of your eyes. Cover your left eye and look at the top hat with your right eye. Bring the book slowly toward your face. You should find that the rabbit suddenly "disappears." This is because light from the rabbit is falling on the blind spot at the back of your eye. There are no light sensors in the blind spot, so you cannot see the rabbit when it is in this position.

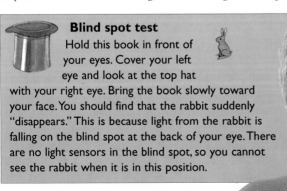

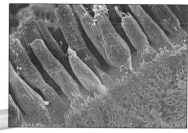

▷ This microscopic view of the retina shows rods (blue) and cones (blue-green). These are light sensors. Rods work in dim light and detect black and white. Cones work in bright light and detect color.

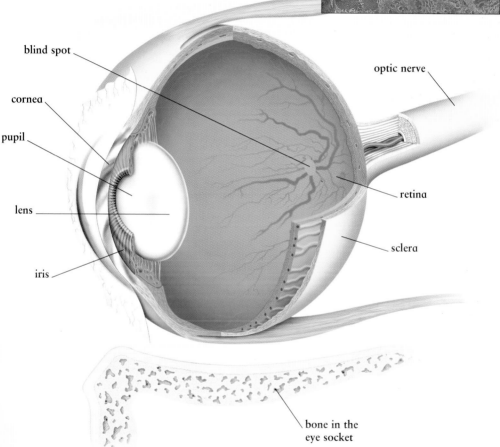

blind spot

cornea

pupil

lens

iris

optic nerve

retina

sclera

bone in the eye socket

△ This cross section of the eye shows its different parts. A tough, white covering called the sclera surrounds the eye. At the front, the clear cornea lets light into the eye. Lining the inside of the back of the eye is the retina. The retina contains light sensors. The blind spot is the place where the optic nerve leaves the eye.

Find Out More

Eye facts
44–45

Touch
50–51

Eye facts

Your eyes are carefully protected. The exposed parts of the eye, not protected by the bony eye sockets, are washed with tears whenever your eyelids blink. Eyelids cover the eyes to protect them from damage, and eyelashes keep dust out. Eyes may not work properly for a number of reasons. Fortunately, there are several ways to fix vision problems.

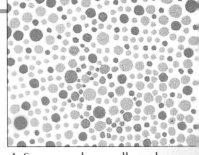

△ Some people, usually males, are color blind. This means they cannot tell certain colors apart. They lack one of the three types of cones (sensors) that detect red, green, or blue light. If you can see the number six in this pattern of dots you are not color-blind.

▷ Blind people cannot use their eyes to read. The Braille reading system allows them to read using touch. Instead of written words, Braille uses patterns of raised dots, in groups of up to six, on paper or cardboard. Sensitive fingertips feel the dot patterns and "read" the words.

◁ Nearsighted people cannot see distant objects clearly. Farsighted people cannot see close objects clearly. In both cases, light is not focused properly inside the eye. Nearsighted and farsighted people can wear glasses or contact lenses to correct their vision.

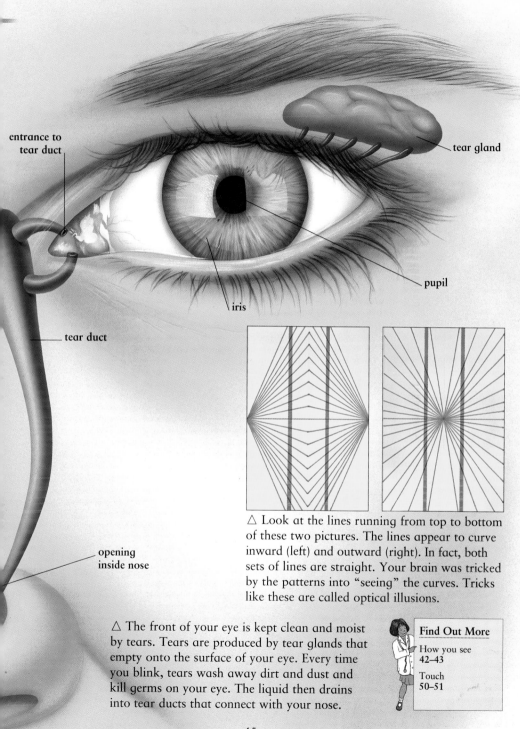

entrance to
tear duct

tear gland

iris

pupil

tear duct

opening
inside nose

△ Look at the lines running from top to bottom of these two pictures. The lines appear to curve inward (left) and outward (right). In fact, both sets of lines are straight. Your brain was tricked by the patterns into "seeing" the curves. Tricks like these are called optical illusions.

△ The front of your eye is kept clean and moist by tears. Tears are produced by tear glands that empty onto the surface of your eye. Every time you blink, tears wash away dirt and dust and kill germs on your eye. The liquid then drains into tear ducts that connect with your nose.

Find Out More

How you see
42–43

Touch
50–51

45

How you hear

From the music of a violin to the roar of a motorcycle, your ears allow you to hear thousands of different sounds. Most of each ear is hidden inside the skull. Sounds travel through the ear until they reach the snail-shaped cochlea. Sensors in the cochlea send nerve messages to the brain so you can hear the sound.

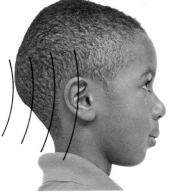

△ Sound travels in waves through the air until it reaches your ears.

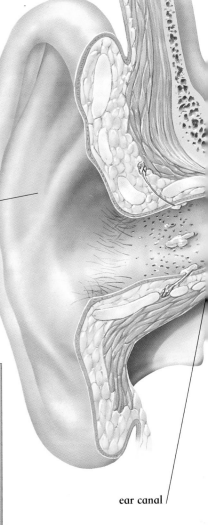

the pinna funnels sound into the ear

ear canal

Balancing act

The semicircular canals in your ears detect the movement and position of your head. This information allows your brain to help you balance. Your brain also receives information from your eyes and feet. Stand on a cushion, put your arms out, raise one leg, and close your eyes. Is it easy to balance?

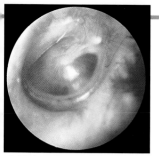

△ Using an instrument called an otoscope, a doctor can examine the ear canal and eardrum inside the ear.

◁ Sound waves send ripples through the liquid in the cochlea. These ripples bend filaments (yellow "v" shapes) that are linked to special cells that send sound messages to the brain.

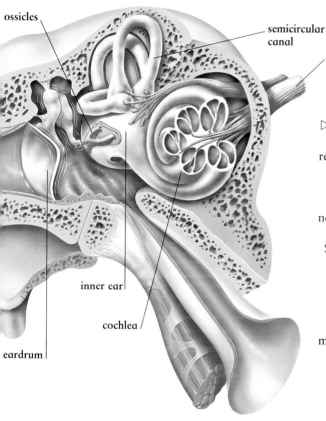

ossicles

semicircular canal

nerve

inner ear

cochlea

eardrum

▷ Have you ever heard a tape recording of your voice? Did it sound the same as your voice normally sounds? Probably not. Sounds from the tape recorder travel to your ears through the air and the skull, which makes your voice sound different.

△ Sound waves hit the eardrum and make it vibrate. These vibrations pass along three tiny bones called the ossicles which create ripples in the fluid filling the inner ear. When these ripples reach the cochlea, it sends messages to the brain.

Find Out More

Touch
50–51

Communication
52–53

Taste and smell

Your senses of taste and smell detect chemicals in food and air. Chemicals in food are detected by sensors called taste buds in your tongue. Chemicals in the air are detected by smell sensors in your nose. The sensors send messages to the brain so that you taste or smell. You can detect many smells, but only four tastes.

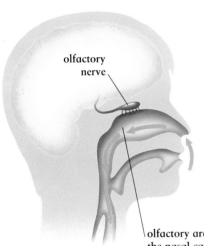

olfactory nerve

olfactory area in the nasal cavity

◁ The nasal cavity carries air to your throat when you breathe in. At the top of the nasal cavity is the olfactory (smelling) area, where sensors pick up smells in the air. The sensors send messages to the brain along the olfactory nerve.

What's that?

Ask an adult to cut different foods, such as an apple and an onion, into bite-size chunks. Blindfold a friend and ask them to hold their nose. Put pieces of food in your friend's mouth. Can they identify them by taste alone?

◁ Your sense of smell warns you about bad odors!

▷ Inside each taste bud is a bundle of sensors that resemble the segments of an orange. When chemicals from food enter the taste bud through an opening called the taste pore, the sensors send messages to the brain.

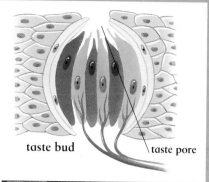

taste bud   **taste pore**

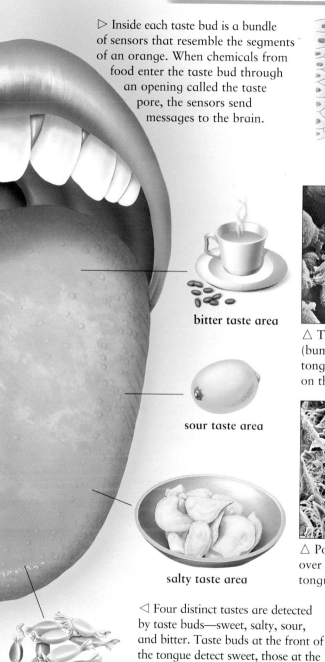

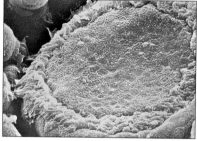

bitter taste area

sour taste area

salty taste area

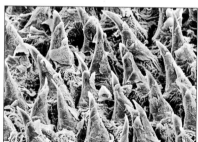

△ This is one of the large papillae (bumps) found at the back of your tongue. Taste buds are located on the sides of these papillae.

△ Pointed papillae are found all over your tongue. They make the tongue rough and help it grip food.

◁ Four distinct tastes are detected by taste buds—sweet, salty, sour, and bitter. Taste buds at the front of the tongue detect sweet, those at the side detect salty and sour, and those **sweet taste area** at the back detect bitter tastes.

Find Out More

Why you eat
70–71

Digesting food
74–75

Touch

Millions of sensors in your skin send a nonstop stream of messages to your brain so that you can touch and feel your surroundings. Some sensors detect light touch, some sense vibrations or pressure, while others sense heat, cold, or pain. Working together, different sensors give your brain a "touch picture."

▽ This view inside the skin shows the different sensors found there. Some lie deep in the dermis, while others reach up into the epidermis. Nerve fibers carry messages from the sensors to the brain.

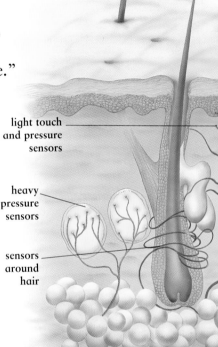

light touch and pressure sensors

heavy pressure sensors

sensors around hair

◁ Some parts of your skin have many more touch sensors than others, making them much more sensitive. This picture of a boy looks odd because the size of his body parts is drawn according to how sensitive they are.

What's that object?

Put some similarly shaped objects, such as a tennis ball, an orange, and a tomato, on a tray. Blindfold a friend and ask them to tell you what each object is by feeling it. Do this again with your friend wearing gloves. How many can they identify now?

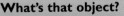

◁ If you put an ice cube in your hand, the sudden temperature drop makes cold sensors send messages to your brain.

◁ This boy is running his fingertips over a piece of sandpaper. As the skin of his fingers is pulled and prodded by the surface of the sandpaper, sensors send messages to his brain. This tells him that sandpaper is rough and covered by thousands of tiny, hard particles.

light pressure sensor

epidermis

dermis

sensor for heat, cold, and pain

△ Sensors for light touch allow you to feel the softness of an animal's fur. At the same time, heat sensors in the skin tell you that the animal is warm as well as soft.

◁ Sensors in the fingers of the boy's right hand sense that a light touch is needed to hold a delicate flower stem. Sensors in the palm of his left hand sense the heavier pressure produced by the vase filled with water.

◁ As you put your clothes on, you feel them rubbing against your skin. This feeling soon disappears. If it did not, you would find wearing clothes very itchy.

Find Out More

Outer covering
14–15

Skin deep
16–17

Communication

People communicate with each other in different ways. Speech allows you to communicate thoughts, ideas, and feelings clearly to other people. Humans are the only animals that can do this. Through body language you can communicate without using words.

▽ Look at these children and their body language. The boy and girl facing one other look interested in what the other is saying. The other boy is being left out.

△ This woman is using sign language to communicate with children who have hearing difficulties. Each position and movement of her fingers and hands means a certain word.

Making sounds

You make sounds using your larynx (voice box). You can feel this by touching the bumpy part in your neck. If you speak or sing, you will feel your larynx vibrate as it produces sounds. Sounds are turned into speech by your tongue and lips. Push your tongue up to the roof of your mouth and try speaking normally.

vocal cords open during normal breathing

vocal cords shut during speech

△ Stretched across the larynx are two folds called vocal cords. Air forced between them as you breathe out makes the vocal cords vibrate and make sounds.

△ When you speak, your brain instructs your tongue and lips to move and change shape in order to form words.

▷ What does this pair's body language tell you? The boy is making a point forcefully, as you can tell from his pointing finger. The girl is protecting herself by folding her arms across her chest.

Find Out More

Learning
38–39

Touch
50–51

Hormones

Hormones are chemical messengers. They are produced by organs called endocrine (or hormonal) glands and are released into the bloodstream. Hormones control many body processes. For example, growth hormones make children grow and sex hormones allow people to reproduce and have babies.

▽ Look at the fear and excitement on the faces of the people on this scary roller coaster ride. In a situation like this, your adrenal glands release the hormone adrenaline. It speeds up your heart and breathing rate so that you are ready to face danger— or run away from it.

◁ Growth hormones make your body grow during childhood. This is why the teenager on the left is much taller than the child on the right.

△ Male sex hormones make hair grow on men's faces.

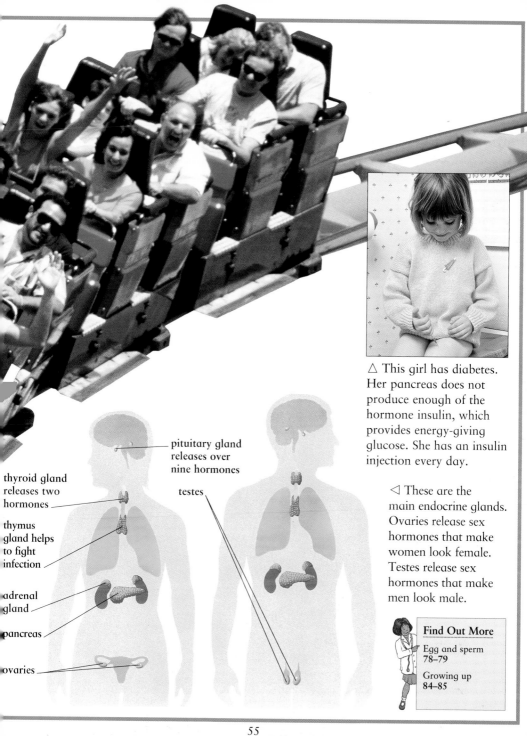

△ This girl has diabetes. Her pancreas does not produce enough of the hormone insulin, which provides energy-giving glucose. She has an insulin injection every day.

pituitary gland releases over nine hormones

thyroid gland releases two hormones

thymus gland helps to fight infection

adrenal gland

pancreas

ovaries

testes

◁ These are the main endocrine glands. Ovaries release sex hormones that make women look female. Testes release sex hormones that make men look male.

Find Out More

Egg and sperm
78–79

Growing up
84–85

Inside the heart

The heart beats over two billion times in a lifetime without stopping. Its job is to pump the blood that supplies your cells with oxygen. The right side of your heart receives blood from your cells and pumps it to the lungs to get oxygen. The left side takes oxygen-rich blood from the lungs and sends it around the body.

▽ Your heart has two sides, and each side has two chambers. The atrium takes blood into the heart, and the ventricle pumps it out. The heart wall is made of strong cardiac muscle. This contracts to produce each heartbeat.

△ In this X ray of the chest of a healthy 11-year-old boy, the heart is yellow and the lungs are dark blue. They are surrounded by protective ribs.

this artery carries blood to the lungs

left atrium

this vein brings in blood from the upper body

right atrium

this vein brings in blood from the lower body

right ventricle

coronary arteries

left ventricle

Listening to heart sounds

If you listen to a friend's chest, your ear will be just a short distance from their heart. If you both stay quiet, you will hear the sounds of their heartbeat. During each beat it makes two sounds, a longer "lubb" sound, followed rapidly by a shorter "dup" sound. The sounds are made by valves in the heart slamming shut to keep blood from flowing in the wrong direction.

◁ The doctor is using a stethoscope to listen to this boy's heart. He listens to the sounds made by the valves in the heart to check that the valves are working properly.

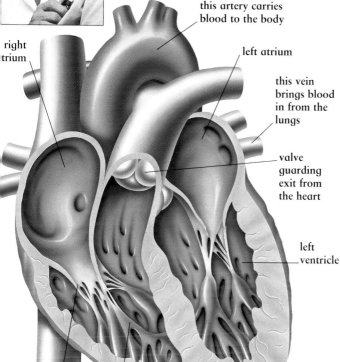

this artery carries blood to the body

right trium

left atrium

this vein brings blood in from the lungs

valve guarding exit from the heart

left ventricle

lve between atrium and ventricle

right ventricle

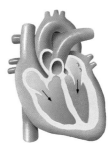

1. The heart relaxes and blood flows into it.

2. The atria contract, pushing blood into the ventricles.

3. The ventricles contract, pushing blood out of the heart.

△ Each heartbeat has three stages: bringing blood into the heart, moving it through, and squeezing it out again.

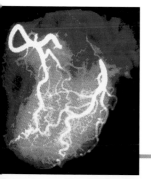

◁ This special X ray of a heart clearly shows the coronary arteries. These keep the muscles in the heart alive by supplying them with food and oxygen. Doctors use X rays like this to look for heart problems caused by blocked coronary arteries.

Find Out More

Blood vessels
58–59

Living liquid
60–61

Blood vessels

Blood vessels are the tubes that carry blood around your body to keep it alive. There are three types of blood vessel. Arteries carry oxygen-rich blood away from your heart. Veins carry oxygen-poor blood back to your heart. Millions of tiny capillaries link the arteries and veins and supply each individual cell with food and oxygen.

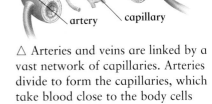

vein

artery   capillary

△ Arteries and veins are linked by a vast network of capillaries. Arteries divide to form the capillaries, which take blood close to the body cells and then join up to form veins.

rest of body   heart   lungs

△ Your body's system of blood vessels has two parts. One carries blood from the heart to the lungs to pick up oxygen. The other carries blood from the heart to all the other body parts to deliver oxygen.

▷ Here you can see the body's main veins. These carry blood from all parts of the body back to your heart. Veins from the legs and abdomen empty into a single large vein that runs up to the heart. Another large vein delivers blood from the head, chest, and arms. Special pulmonary veins carry oxygen-rich blood from the lungs around to the left side of the heart.

main vein from upper body to the heart

pulmonary veins bring oxygen-rich blood back from the lungs

heart

main vein from lower body to the heart

this vein carries blood back from the leg

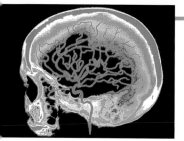

△ This X ray of the head shows the branching carotid artery. The carotid arteries supply blood to your brain.

Measuring your pulse
Use two fingertips to feel the inside of your wrist, just below your thumb. Can you feel your pulse? This is caused by an artery under the skin bulging out when your heart beats. Count the number of pulse beats in 10 seconds. Ask a friend to time you. Multiply the number by six. This is your number of heartbeats per minute.

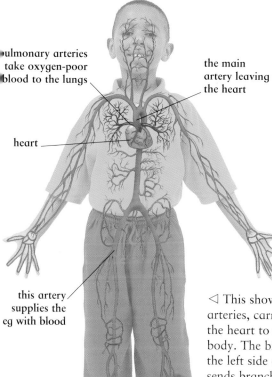

pulmonary arteries take oxygen-poor blood to the lungs

the main artery leaving the heart

heart

this artery supplies the leg with blood

△ This is a microscopic view of the inside of a tiny capillary. You can see a mass of densely packed red blood cells traveling through it. Capillaries pass very close to body cells. As this happens, the red blood cells give their oxygen to the cells.

◁ This shows the body's main arteries, carrying blood from the heart to all parts of the body. The biggest artery leaves the left side of the heart and sends branches to the head, arms, chest, and legs. As arteries branch out, they get smaller until they become capillaries. Special pulmonary arteries carry oxygen-poor blood from the heart to the lungs.

Find Out More

Living liquid
60–61

How you breathe
66–67

Living liquid

Blood is the body's liquid delivery and removal service. It is made up of four parts. Plasma delivers food to all your body's cells, while platelets help to heal wounds. Red blood cells carry oxygen to your cells and remove their waste. White blood cells play a vital part in your body's defense against germs.

▷ This woman is giving blood. A needle is inserted into a vein in her arm and about a pint of blood is collected. Her blood can later be given to someone who has lost blood in an accident or in an operation.

△ This is a blood sample that has been separated into its two main parts. Red blood cells are at the bottom and plasma is on top.

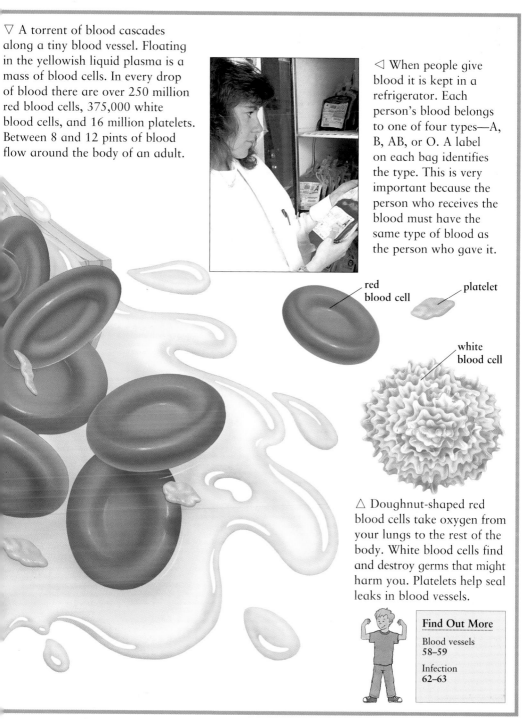

▽ A torrent of blood cascades along a tiny blood vessel. Floating in the yellowish liquid plasma is a mass of blood cells. In every drop of blood there are over 250 million red blood cells, 375,000 white blood cells, and 16 million platelets. Between 8 and 12 pints of blood flow around the body of an adult.

◁ When people give blood it is kept in a refrigerator. Each person's blood belongs to one of four types—A, B, AB, or O. A label on each bag identifies the type. This is very important because the person who receives the blood must have the same type of blood as the person who gave it.

red blood cell

platelet

white blood cell

△ Doughnut-shaped red blood cells take oxygen from your lungs to the rest of the body. White blood cells find and destroy germs that might harm you. Platelets help seal leaks in blood vessels.

Find Out More

Blood vessels
58–59

Infection
62–63

Infection

Germs, such as bacteria and viruses, are always trying to get inside your body. If they do, they can infect you and cause diseases. Luckily, your body has many defenses. Skin forms a barrier against germs, but if some manage to get through, white blood cells hunt them down and destroy them.

▽ A white blood cell called a "cell-eater" has tracked down its prey. This is a germ that is attempting to infect the human body and cause disease. The cell-eater wraps itself around the germ, and destroys the germ by digesting it.

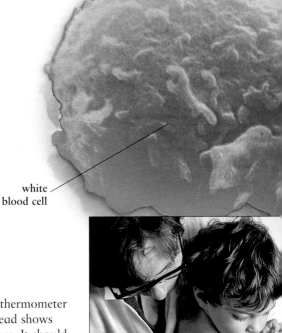

white blood cell

△ This is a microscopic view of bacteria on the surface of the skin. These germs are harmless on the skin, but if they get inside your body, through cuts or down the throat, they can infect you and make you sick.

◁ The heat-sensitive thermometer strip on this boy's head shows his body temperature. It should be about 98.6°F. If it is higher, he could be sick. The body uses high temperature to kill germs. A very high temperature is called a fever.

△ A doctor gives a boy a vaccine to protect him from a particular germ. The vaccine makes his body produce special chemicals to kill the germ if it attacks him.

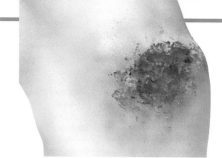

◁ Cut skin lets in germs. If you cut your skin, the body acts quickly to seal broken blood vessels and repair the damage. The blood clots, or thickens, and then dries, leaving a scab like this one. Under the scab the healing process continues until the skin is repaired.

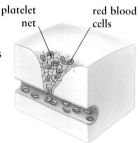

platelet net   red blood cells

▷ When a cut in the skin breaks a blood vessel, platelets in the blood form a "net" that traps red blood cells.

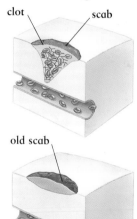

clot   scab

▷ The trapped red blood cells make a clot that plugs the wound. The surface of the clot hardens to form a scab.

old scab

▷ Beneath the scab, the skin and the blood vessel repair themselves. Finally, the old, dry scab drops off.

invading germ

◁ This boy has scraped his knee. His mother washes the wound with a cotton ball soaked in antiseptic liquid. This removes dirt and kills germs, so there is less chance of them invading the body.

Find Out More

Skin deep
16–17

Living liquid
60–61

Why you breathe

You need to breathe in air because it contains oxygen. Every cell in your body uses oxygen to release the energy from food that keeps your cells (and you!) alive. Oxygen is taken from the air by your breathing system—your nose, throat, windpipe, and lungs. Inside the lungs, oxygen passes into the blood.

▷ The two lungs in your chest are linked to the outside by the windpipe. This opens into your throat. Lungs are soft and spongy, because they are made of a mass of tubes and tiny air bags. Blood flows through them constantly to pick up oxygen.

windpipe

right lung

△ There is little oxygen under water, so your lungs cannot work properly. To keep your body from running out of oxygen when you go diving you have to carry your own air supply in tanks, like this woman swimming along a coral reef.

Catch your breath

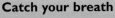

Take a mirror and hold it right in front of your mouth. Now breathe out onto the surface of the mirror. What happens? You should find that a fine mist of water droplets has formed on the mirror. The insides of your lungs are moist. When you breathe out, the moist air forms the tiny droplets on the mirror.

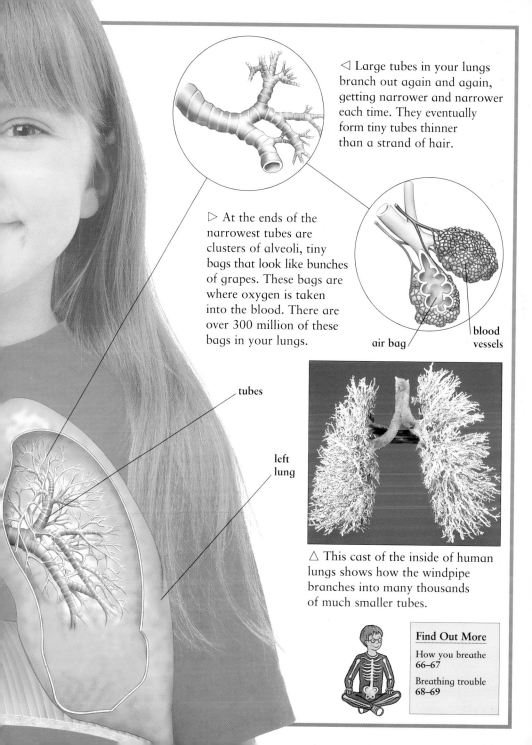

◁ Large tubes in your lungs branch out again and again, getting narrower and narrower each time. They eventually form tiny tubes thinner than a strand of hair.

▷ At the ends of the narrowest tubes are clusters of alveoli, tiny bags that look like bunches of grapes. These bags are where oxygen is taken into the blood. There are over 300 million of these bags in your lungs.

air bag

blood vessels

tubes

left lung

△ This cast of the inside of human lungs shows how the windpipe branches into many thousands of much smaller tubes.

Find Out More

How you breathe 66–67

Breathing trouble 68–69

How you breathe

Every time you breathe, you move air in and out of your lungs. This makes sure that life-giving oxygen gets to the lungs, while waste carbon dioxide is removed. But your lungs cannot move on their own. Breathing depends on your ribs and diaphragm, a sheet of muscle under the lungs. They make your lungs suck in and squeeze out air through your nose and mouth.

ribs move upward and outward

diaphragm moves downward

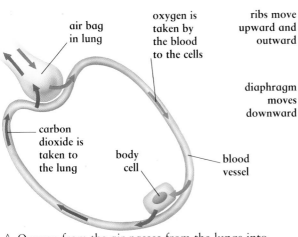

air bag in lung

oxygen is taken by the blood to the cells

carbon dioxide is taken to the lung

body cell

blood vessel

△ Oxygen from the air passes from the lungs into the blood. The blood then carries oxygen to the body's cells, picks up waste carbon dioxide, and carries this back to the lungs, where it is breathed out.

▷ To breathe in, the muscles between your ribs pull the ribs up and out, and your diaphragm moves down. This makes more space in your chest, and air is sucked into your lungs. When you breathe out, your rib muscles move down, and your diaphragm moves up. This reduces the space in your chest, and air is squeezed from your lungs.

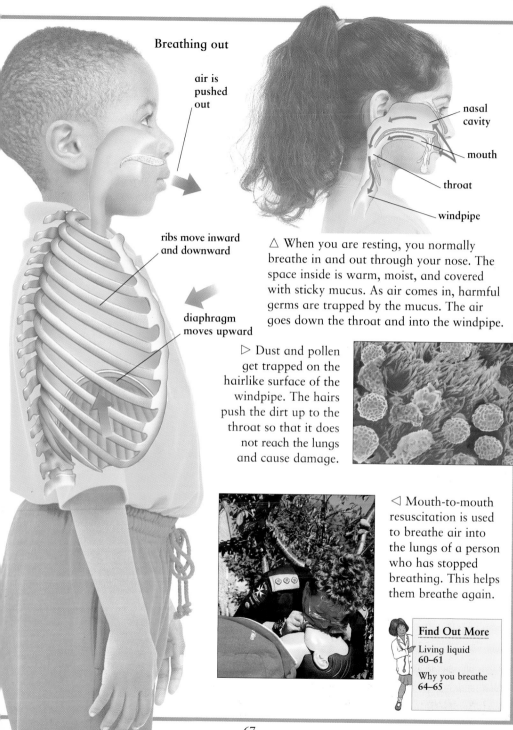

Breathing out

air is pushed out

nasal cavity

mouth

throat

windpipe

ribs move inward and downward

diaphragm moves upward

△ When you are resting, you normally breathe in and out through your nose. The space inside is warm, moist, and covered with sticky mucus. As air comes in, harmful germs are trapped by the mucus. The air goes down the throat and into the windpipe.

▷ Dust and pollen get trapped on the hairlike surface of the windpipe. The hairs push the dirt up to the throat so that it does not reach the lungs and cause damage.

◁ Mouth-to-mouth resuscitation is used to breathe air into the lungs of a person who has stopped breathing. This helps them breathe again.

Find Out More

Living liquid 60–61

Why you breathe 64–65

Breathing trouble

Most of the time you breathe in and out regularly. Sometimes this is interrupted, by sneezes, yawns, coughs, or hiccups. When you sneeze, air rushes from your lungs and bursts out through your nose to clear away any irritations. The droplets released by sneezing can pass disease from one person to another.

▽ When you sneeze, a jet of droplets shoots out of your nose and mouth, faster than a speeding car. Sneezes are triggered by dust, pollen, or by the sticky mucus produced when you get a cold. Air from the lungs builds up in the windpipe and is then released to blast out the irritation.

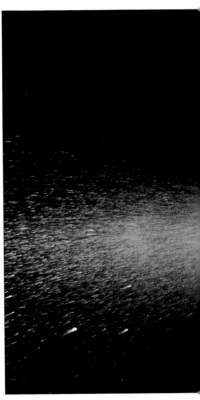

◁ Like many people, this girl gets hay fever in the summer months. She is sensitive to pollen grains that she has breathed in. The pollen irritates her, and gives her a sore throat, itchy eyes, and a runny nose.

▷ This is a microscopic view of pollen grains. Millions of grains are produced by flowers in order to reproduce. Pollen grains cause hay fever when they are breathed in by certain people.

▷ This boy has asthma and is using an inhaler. Asthma makes it difficult to breathe because the small tubes in the lungs suddenly get narrower when irritated. The medicine from the inhaler opens the tubes up again.

◁ Pollution means that there is something dirty in your surroundings that should not be there. In the modern world, pollution of the air you breathe is caused by gases and tiny dust particles produced by factories and cars. This pollution may be the reason why more and more people are developing asthma and other breathing problems.

△ These are human lungs. The top picture shows the lungs of a person who never smoked. The bottom picture shows the lungs of a heavy smoker who died of lung cancer. The black marks are produced by cigarette smoke. Cigarettes are the main cause of lung cancer.

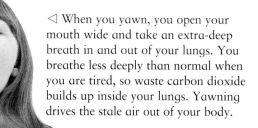

◁ When you yawn, you open your mouth wide and take an extra-deep breath in and out of your lungs. You breathe less deeply than normal when you are tired, so waste carbon dioxide builds up inside your lungs. Yawning drives the stale air out of your body.

Find Out More

Why you breathe
64–65

When you are sick
94–95

Why you eat

Just as a car needs gas to keep moving, you need food to keep your body working properly. Food contains useful substances called nutrients. Nutrients provide energy and building materials for growth and repair. For you to use these nutrients, your food must first be digested, or broken down into smaller pieces.

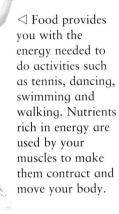

◁ Food provides you with the energy needed to do activities such as tennis, dancing, swimming and walking. Nutrients rich in energy are used by your muscles to make them contract and move your body.

◁ Nearly two thirds of your body is made up of water. You lose water when you go to the bathroom or sweat. Lost water has to be replaced. You take in water when you drink and when you eat.

Digesting bread

Take a piece of bread and put it in your mouth. Chew it for a few minutes before swallowing it. At first the bread has little taste, but after some chewing it tastes sweet. This is because the saliva (spit) inside your mouth contains an enzyme (digesting chemical). It digests the starch in bread by turning it into sweet sugars.

△ Whether you are lying down or standing up, fast asleep or wide awake, your body is constantly making use of the food you eat and digest. After being digested, food is carried to all your body cells by blood. As nutrients are used up by the cells, your brain detects that the level of nutrients in your blood is going down. When this happens you start to feel hungry and eat more food.

◁ From the time you are born until your body is growing. The various nutrients in food play different roles in the growing process. Some act as the building blocks that are used to make your muscles, bones, and other body parts develop. Others provide the constant supply of energy needed to make you grow. To make sure you grow properly, it is important to eat a mixed, healthy diet.

△ Your body is constantly repairing itself. Its ability to do this is easy to see when you break your arm. The bones in your arm rebuild themselves. All these repair processes need nutrients from the food you eat.

◁ This blender shows what happens to food during digestion. On the left, the blender contains bite-size chunks of food. On the right, the blender has broken down the food chunks into a soup.

Find Out More

All about teeth
72–73

Digesting food
74–75

All about teeth

Your teeth cut and crush food into small pieces so it can be swallowed and digested. There are four main types of teeth. Incisors slide past each other to cut up food. Pointed canines grip and pierce food, and flat-topped premolars and molars crush food. During a lifetime, a person has two sets of teeth—baby teeth and adult teeth.

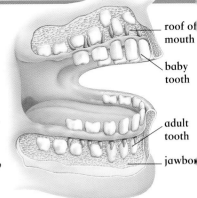

roof of mouth

baby tooth

adult tooth

jawbon

△ During childhood, your 20 baby teeth are pushed out of your gums and replaced by adult teeth.

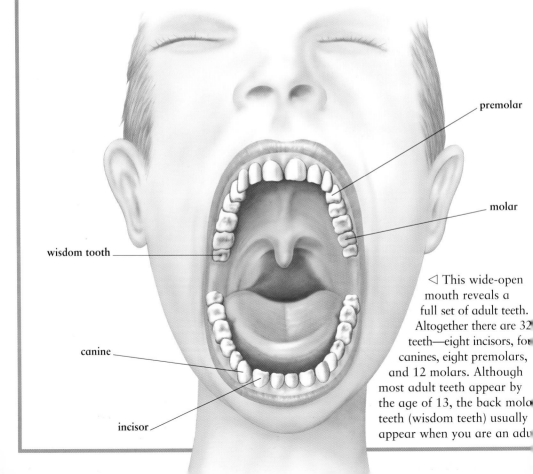

premolar

molar

wisdom tooth

canine

incisor

◁ This wide-open mouth reveals a full set of adult teeth. Altogether there are 32 teeth—eight incisors, for canines, eight premolars, and 12 molars. Although most adult teeth appear by the age of 13, the back mola teeth (wisdom teeth) usually appear when you are an adu

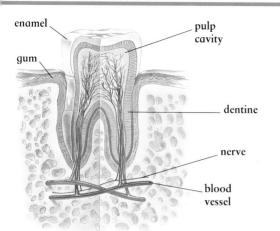

enamel
pulp cavity
gum
dentine
nerve
blood vessel

△ A tooth has a covering of hard, white enamel. Inside, a bony dentine layer surrounds the inner pulp cavity with its blood vessels and nerve endings.

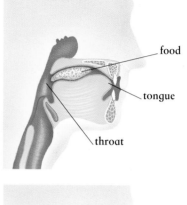

food
tongue
throat

▷ It is important to clean your teeth thoroughly two or three times each day. Brushing removes leftover food and helps prevent tooth decay.

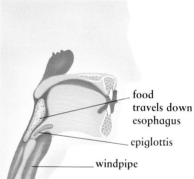

food travels down esophagus
epiglottis
windpipe

△ The tongue pushes chewed food to the back of your throat and sets off the automatic process of swallowing. A flap called the epiglottis covers your windpipe as you swallow. This keeps food from going down the wrong way and making you choke.

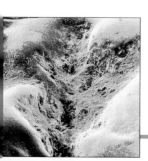

◁ This molar is covered with plaque, a mixture of food and bacteria which builds up if teeth are not cleaned. It releases acids that cause tooth decay.

Find Out More

Why you eat
70–71

Digesting food
74–75

Digesting food

Before your body can use the food you eat, it needs to digest it—to break it down into simple nutrients. Food is crushed to a paste in your stomach, then digested in your small intestine by special chemicals called enzymes. The nutrients pass through the wall of the small intestine into your blood. Any waste matter travels along your large intestine and out through your anus.

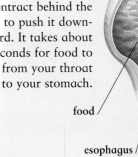

muscles contract

▷ After swallowing, the chewed food is squeezed down your esophagus. Muscles in the esophagus wall contract behind the food to push it down-ward. It takes about five seconds for food to move from your throat to your stomach.

food

esophagus

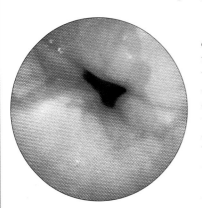

◁ The esophagus connects your mouth to your stomach. This view of the esophagus at the stomach entrance is produced using an instrument called an endoscope. The walls of the esophagus are smooth and slimy so that food can slip down easily.

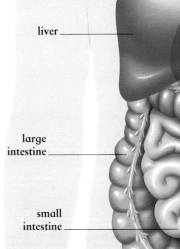

liver

large intestine

small intestine

Food journey

Take a long sock and put a tennis ball inside one end of it. Hold the end of the sock with one hand and grip the sock just behind the ball with the other. Now squeeze with your fingers to push the ball so that it slides along the sock. This action is similar to what happens when food travels down your esophagus.

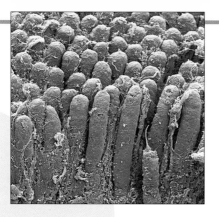

◁ This microscopic view inside the small intestine looks like a forest of little fingers. These fingers are called villi, and each one is about $\frac{1}{25}$ inch long. Nutrients from digested food pass through these villi in the small intestine into your bloodstream.

esophagus

▷ Inside your large intestine there are millions of germs called bacteria. Normally they are harmless, but if you get the bacteria on your fingers and then touch your food, they can make you sick. That is why it is important to wash your hands after going to the bathroom.

stomach

pancreas

◁ When you need to get rid of waste matter (feces), you go to the bathroom. Babies cannot control when they release feces so they need to wear a diaper that is changed regularly.

◁ Your digestive system is basically a long tube that runs from your mouth to your anus. In the stomach, swallowed food is stored for a few hours, churned up, and partially digested. Digestion finishes in the small intestine, with the help of liquids from the liver and pancreas. Undigested food dries out as it passes along the large intestine and forms brown feces.

rectum

anus

Find Out More

Why you eat
70–71

All about teeth
72–73

75

Waste disposal

Millions of chemical processes go on inside your body's cells. These processes release waste into your blood that would poison you if you did not get rid of it. The job of disposing of this waste is carried out by the urinary system which filters waste and excess water from your blood to make urine. The urine is released when you go to the bathroom.

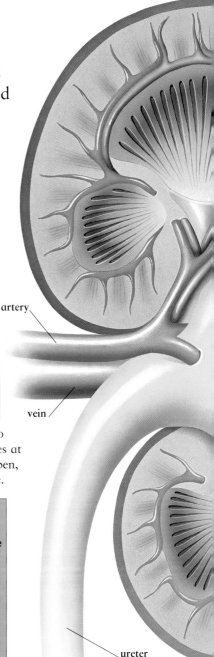

artery

vein

ureter

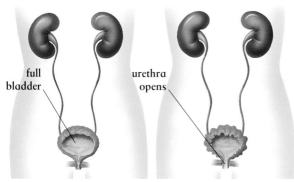

full bladder

urethra opens

△ As the bladder fills, it sends messages to the brain so that you feel a need to go to the bathroom. The muscles at the bottom of the bladder relax, making the urethra open, and the bladder walls contract to squeeze out the urine.

Kidney sieve
Mix together some salt and sugar and shake it in a sieve over a bowl. The salt passes through the sieve while the sugar stays in it. Your kidneys sift blood so that you lose waste, but keep nutrients.

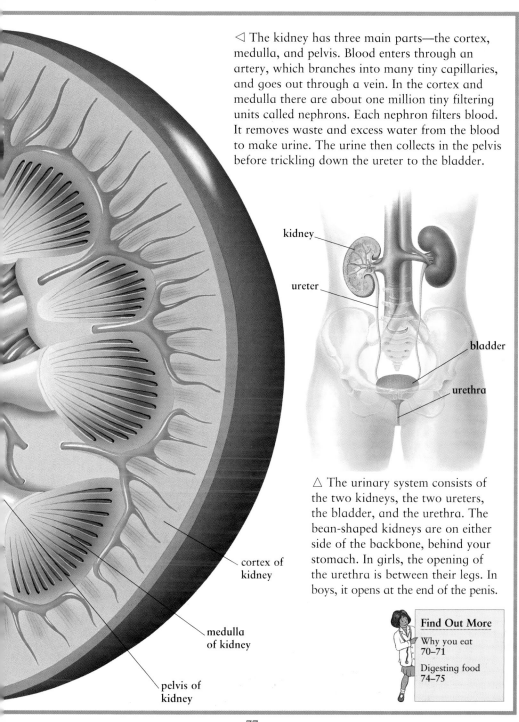

◁ The kidney has three main parts—the cortex, medulla, and pelvis. Blood enters through an artery, which branches into many tiny capillaries, and goes out through a vein. In the cortex and medulla there are about one million tiny filtering units called nephrons. Each nephron filters blood. It removes waste and excess water from the blood to make urine. The urine then collects in the pelvis before trickling down the ureter to the bladder.

kidney

ureter

bladder

urethra

△ The urinary system consists of the two kidneys, the two ureters, the bladder, and the urethra. The bean-shaped kidneys are on either side of the backbone, behind your stomach. In girls, the opening of the urethra is between their legs. In boys, it opens at the end of the penis.

cortex of kidney

medulla of kidney

pelvis of kidney

Find Out More

Why you eat 70–71

Digesting food 74–75

Egg and sperm

Adult humans use their reproductive systems to make babies. Males produce cells called sperm that can swim. Females produce a single egg each month. To make a baby, a man puts his penis inside a woman's vagina to release sperm. The sperm swim toward the egg and fertilize it. The fertilized egg grows into a baby inside the uterus.

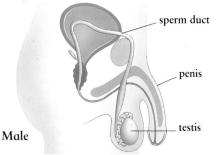

Male

sperm duct

penis

testis

△ Millions of sperm are made in the testes every day. They travel along the sperm duct and out through the penis.

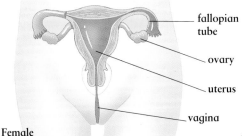

fallopian tube

ovary

uterus

vagina

Female

△ The ovaries release an egg each month. An egg is fertilized if it meets a sperm as it travels along a fallopian tube to the uterus.

△ A mass of sperm surrounds an egg as it travels along the fallopian tube. Each sperm tries to break through the outer layer of the egg to fertilize it. They all release chemicals to dissolve the outer layer. Only one sperm will manage to get through.

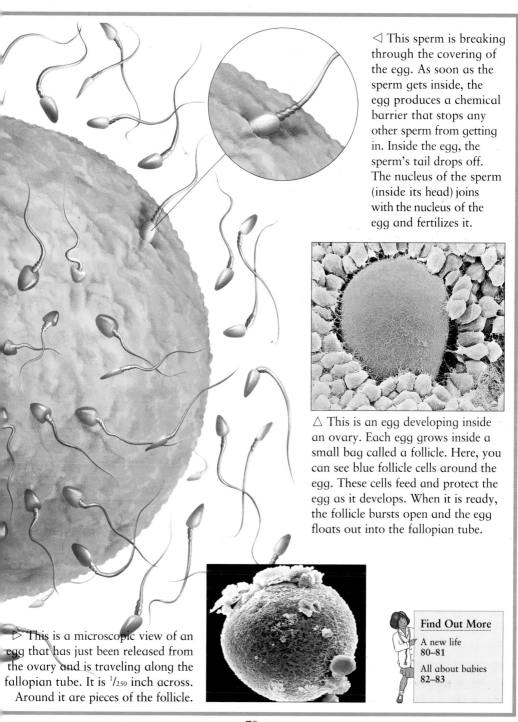

◁ This sperm is breaking through the covering of the egg. As soon as the sperm gets inside, the egg produces a chemical barrier that stops any other sperm from getting in. Inside the egg, the sperm's tail drops off. The nucleus of the sperm (inside its head) joins with the nucleus of the egg and fertilizes it.

△ This is an egg developing inside an ovary. Each egg grows inside a small bag called a follicle. Here, you can see blue follicle cells around the egg. These cells feed and protect the egg as it develops. When it is ready, the follicle bursts open and the egg floats out into the fallopian tube.

▷ This is a microscopic view of an egg that has just been released from the ovary and is traveling along the fallopian tube. It is $1/250$ inch across. Around it are pieces of the follicle.

Find Out More

A new life
80–81

All about babies
82–83

79

A new life

If a sperm fertilizes an egg inside a woman, a new life is produced. The fertilized egg divides to produce a hollow ball of cells that settles in the uterus. Over the next nine months, this ball of cells will develop into a baby. The developing baby is linked to its mother by the umbilical cord. Food and oxygen pass from the mother to the baby along the cord.

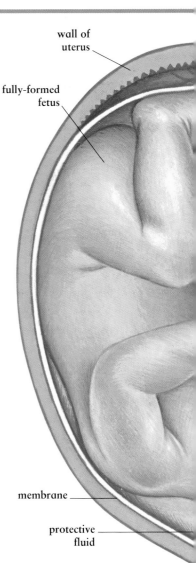

wall of uterus

fully-formed fetus

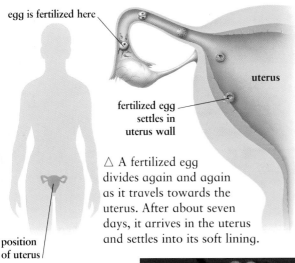

egg is fertilized here

uterus

fertilized egg settles in uterus wall

position of uterus

△ A fertilized egg divides again and again as it travels towards the uterus. After about seven days, it arrives in the uterus and settles into its soft lining.

membrane

protective fluid

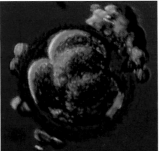

▷ Two days after fertilization, the single cell of the fertilized egg has divided to become four cells. These cells will keep dividing until they become the billions of cells that make up a human body.

▷ This baby is between 38 and 40 weeks old, and is ready to be born. A few weeks earlier it turned upside down, so it will be born head first. During birth, the muscular wall of the uterus starts to contract. The membrane around the baby breaks, and the uterus squeezes the baby out through the vagina.

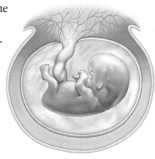

◁ At five weeks, the baby is about the size of an apple seed. It has a tail that will soon disappear. Buds are forming that will become the arms and legs, and the heart is just starting to beat.

▷ At eight weeks, the developing baby is called a fetus. It is as big as a strawberry. You can see its eyes, ears, and tiny developing fingers and toes.

umbilical cord

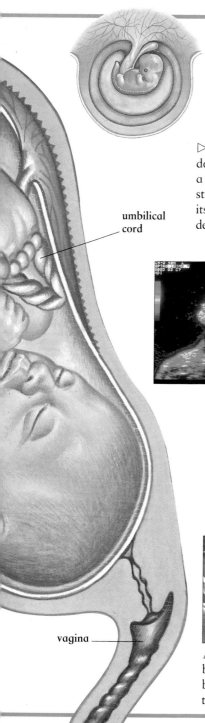

◁ This ultrasound scan of a woman's uterus shows a 22-week-old fetus. You can see its head and face clearly. Doctors use ultrasound scans as a safe way of checking that the fetus is healthy.

▷ This woman is pregnant. That means that she is expecting a baby. You can tell she is pregnant because the growing fetus inside her uterus is making her abdomen bulge outward.

vagina

△ This baby has just been born and taken her first breath. She is still attached to the umbilical cord.

Find Out More

All about babies
82–83

Growing up
84–85

All about babies

Newborn babies are helpless and completely dependent on their parents. At first they are fed only on milk, but after a few months they start eating solid food. Young babies sleep most of the time, but soon they spend more and more time exploring. In this way, they learn how the world around them works.

△ The world is an exciting place for a baby. There is so much to learn. By pulling on a toy telephone, the baby feels the hardness of plastic and learns how to make something move. Crawling on all fours makes exploring even easier.

◁ Babies form a close bond with their parents. Being held and cuddled plays an important part in making a baby feel happy and secure. The baby responds to its parents by smiling, gurgling, and making other noises. Although they may not understand, babies love to hear talking and singing. Gradually, they learn to speak themselves.

▷ This baby was born six weeks early and needs special care. He is in an incubator in a hospital. The baby is kept warm and his breathing and heart rate are checked regularly by nurses. The baby's parents can touch him through holes in the incubator.

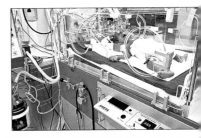

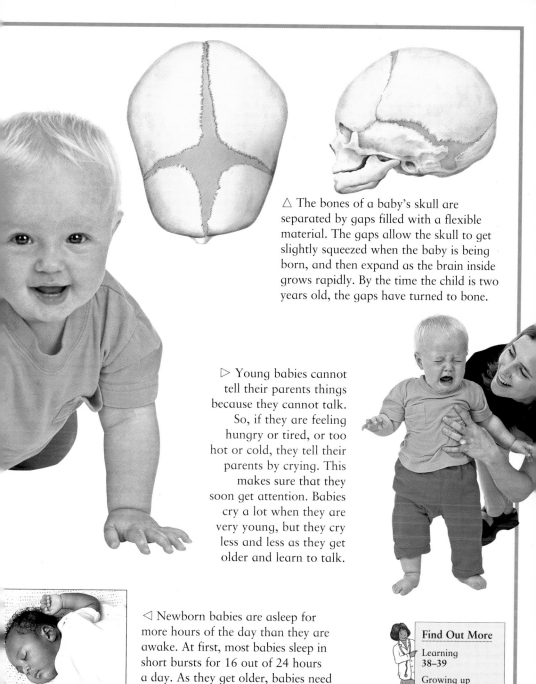

△ The bones of a baby's skull are separated by gaps filled with a flexible material. The gaps allow the skull to get slightly squeezed when the baby is being born, and then expand as the brain inside grows rapidly. By the time the child is two years old, the gaps have turned to bone.

▷ Young babies cannot tell their parents things because they cannot talk. So, if they are feeling hungry or tired, or too hot or cold, they tell their parents by crying. This makes sure that they soon get attention. Babies cry a lot when they are very young, but they cry less and less as they get older and learn to talk.

◁ Newborn babies are asleep for more hours of the day than they are awake. At first, most babies sleep in short bursts for 16 out of 24 hours a day. As they get older, babies need less sleep, and start to sleep more at night than during the day.

Find Out More

Learning
38–39

Growing up
84–85

83

Growing up

Everyone grows up in the same way. During the first year after birth, the body grows very quickly. Through the rest of childhood, growth is slow and steady, as children develop the skills that they will need as adults. Finally, in the early teens, growth speeds up again as children become adults. As adults, men and women no longer grow.

◁ When he is nearly a year old, this infant can sit up, crawl, and pull himself onto his feet by holding on to a chair. His head is still fairly large compared to the rest of his body.

▷ This two-year-old child is busy learning by playing with some colored plastic shapes. She is able to walk and climb stairs and is learning to talk. She can also draw simple pictures.

◁ This eight-year-old can ride a bicycle and perform many other skilled actions. She is able to read and write clearly and accurately, and can speak using a wide range of words.

◁ These two teenagers have reached puberty. This is a time of rapid growth when children start to look like adult men and women. It is also the time when their reproductive systems start working, so they can have children. Puberty usually happens between the ages of about 10 and 16 and begins earlier in girls than boys. By the age of 20, growth comes to an end.

◁ In their 20s and 30s, many men and women get married and have children. They now have to spend much of their time looking after their children, and continue to do so until the children leave home.

▷ By their 40s and 50s, most men and women show signs of getting older. Very slowly, their bodies become less efficient at doing things.

△ As people get older, their skin wrinkles, their hair turns gray, and their bodies become less strong.

Find Out More

Family tree
86–87

Similarities
88–89

Family tree

In every family, there are similarities between parents and their children. This is because when men and women have children, they pass on tiny packages of information called chromosomes in their egg and sperm. These are the instructions that will make a unique new person, who will have some of the features of both parents, as well as many of their own.

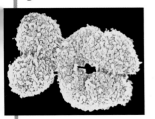

◁ This is one of the chromosomes found inside each of your body's cells. Chromosomes carry information that controls body features, such as the color of your eyes.

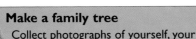

▷ These girls are identical twins. Their cells contain identical chromosomes. When their mother's egg was fertilized, it split into two halves, and each developed into a girl.

Make a family tree

Collect photographs of yourself, your parents, any brothers or sisters, grandparents, and even great-grandparents. Now arrange them on the page with you at the bottom, your parents above you, and your grandparents above them. Look at the photos. Can you see any similarities that have been passed on from one generation to the next?

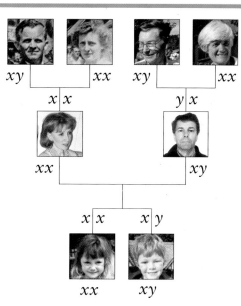

$\triangle$ Two of the chromosomes inside each of your cells control whether you are a girl or a boy. They are called the sex chromosomes. There are two types, X and Y. Boys have one X and one Y chromosome, while girls have two X chromosomes. A man's sperm can carry either an X or a Y chromosome, but a woman's egg can only contain an X chromosome. If an X-carrying sperm fertilizes an egg, a girl (XX) is produced. If a Y-carrying sperm fertilizes the egg, a boy (XY) is produced.

$\triangleleft$ Here are three generations of one family. The man on the left is the father of the woman, and grandfather of the two children. The children's father is standing on the right. See if you can spot any similarities between the generations.

Find Out More

Egg and sperm
78–79

Similarities
88–89

Similarities

Look at people in the street, and you will notice many differences. But look again and see if you can spot the similarities—such as the way people shrug their shoulders, frown when they are thinking, wave good-bye, or laugh at a joke. You will see behavior like this all around the world.

▽ A crowd of children play in a playground in Cuba. Although each child moves, shouts, and laughs in exactly the same way as you, they all have their own personality. Some are girls and some are boys. Some have lighter skin and some have darker skin, and they may speak a different language from you. These differences add variety and interest to all our lives.

▷ Find a picture of yourself and glue it here. You have taken your place in this gallery of human beings!

Your picture goes here

◁ This boy is unable to walk and has to use a wheelchair to get around—and do his homework in. Having this, or any other disability, should not stop people from living their lives to the fullest.

◁ These athletes race in their high-speed wheelchairs with the same urge to win as able-bodied athletes. We all have the same ability to succeed, if given the opportunity.

◁ These children are playing in a back street in Morocco. All children play, whether they live in a big city or a village in the middle of a rain forest. Playing together lets children practice the skills they will need when they grow up.

▷ This is a child from Nepal, in the foothills of the Himalayas. His skin color and the shape of his face may differ from yours, but his smile is a sign of greeting and of happiness that would be recognized anywhere in the world.

△ People everywhere enjoy playing games. These Brazilian boys do not own a set of checkers, so they use bottle caps instead.

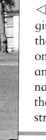

◁ Two Australian girls go walking in the afternoon sun. The one with darker hair and skin has greater natural protection from the harmful effects of strong sunlight.

Find Out More

Our bodies
10–11

Growing up
84–85

89

Staying fit

A fit body is one that can perform everyday tasks without getting tired and breathless. Staying fit helps people stay healthy into old age. Fitness depends on eating a balanced diet and exercising regularly. There are three types of fitness—flexibility, stamina, and strength.

▽ Stretching and bending keeps your body in good shape. First, it helps your body warm up before you start to exercise. If your muscles are warm, they work more efficiently. Second, stretching and bending makes your body more flexible so that your muscles and joints can move more freely.

△ These young ballet dancers are being taught exercises. Dancers have to be very flexible to perform all their movements. They need strength to hold positions, and stamina to perform without getting tired.

◁ Swimming is one of the best all-around exercises. The movement of your arms and legs strengthens your muscles. Because your weight is supported by the water as you stretch out, swimming is great for flexibility. Regular swimming also increases your stamina.

△ Push-ups strengthen your arms and shoulders as well as the muscles in your abdomen, back, and legs. Every time you do a push-up, your arms have to support the weight of your body.

△ Basketball keeps you fit by boosting your stamina. It makes you stretch every time you pass the ball or shoot a basket, and your arms and legs get stronger.

◁ This boy spends a lot of time watching television and eating fatty foods. He is overweight because he does not get much exercise and consumes more energy than his body actually needs.

Find Out More

Muscle power
26–27

Healthy food
92–93

Healthy food

Food is made up of nutrients that give your body the energy it needs to move, and the building materials that make you grow. You need a variety of these nutrients to help keep you fit and healthy. This is called a balanced diet. The food pyramid shows what to eat to get the balance right.

▷ Fats keep you warm, but you should only eat a small amount. They are at the top of the food pyramid because you need less of them than other foods.

▷ Dairy products, such as milk, provide calcium, which is needed for strong teeth and bones. Milk is healthier than sugary soft drinks.

▷ Foods rich in protein are essential for the body to grow and repair itself. Beans, fish, chicken, meat, and cheese are all good sources of protein. Meat and cheese also contain a lot of fat.

▷ Fresh fruit and vegetables provide you with fiber, as well as plenty of vitamins and minerals. Fiber keeps your digestion working smoothly. Vitamins and minerals are essential for good health.

▷ Foods rich in carbohydrates should make up most of your diet. Rice, bread, potatoes, and pasta are all rich in starchy carbohydrates. These release their energy slowly and keep you fueled up throughout the day.

△ This meal is not well-balanced. It contains a lot of fat and salt, and hardly any fiber or vitamins.

Keep a food diary
Try keeping a food diary to see whether or not you are eating a balanced diet. For two days, write down everthing you eat at each meal. Using the food pyramid, write down what nutrients each meal contains. Are your meals balanced, or do they contain a lot of fat and sugar? Use your diary to think about how you might improve your diet.

◁ A baked potato is a good source of energy because it is packed with starchy carbohydrates. Unlike french fries, which are fried in oil, baked potatoes contain very little fat.

▷ In many parts of the world, people get the carbohydrates they need from rice. In India, for example, it is eaten with curry. The vegetables give you fiber, vitamins, and minerals, and the lentils contain protein.

Find Out More

Why you eat
70–71

Digesting food
74–75

When you are sick

Sometimes, parts of the body stop working properly and we get sick. This may happen because the body becomes infected by germs from outside, or because something is damaged inside the body. Doctors do tests and use their knowledge and experience to find out what is wrong with their patients.

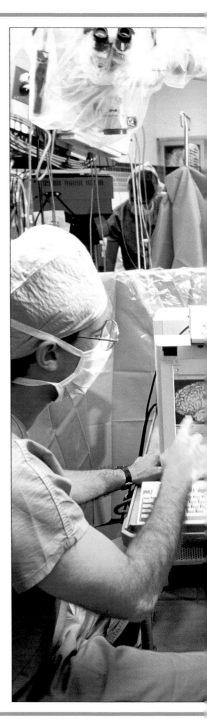

◁ This girl has a thermometer in her mouth, under her tongue. It will stay there for a few minutes to measure the temperature inside her body. Normally this should be about 98.6°F. If she is sick, her temperature may go up.

△ This doctor is measuring his patient's blood pressure. Blood pressure is produced by the heart when it beats. It measures how strongly blood is pushed along the arteries. If this woman's pressure is too high or too low, she may need treatment.

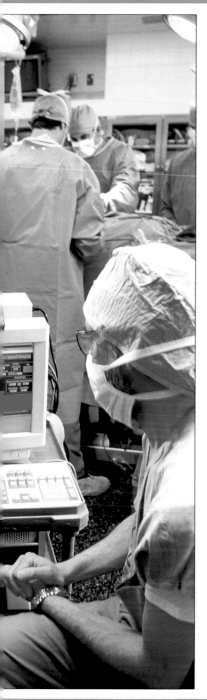

▷ This X ray shows that the bones in the forearm are broken. X rays allow doctors to look inside a person's body. This patient's arm will be put in a plaster cast that allows the bones to repair themselves.

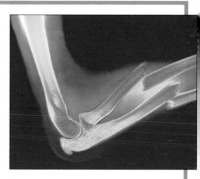

◁ Wounds in the skin are usually covered with a dressing or bandage. This protects the wound from any bacteria in the air or on the skin that might get into the wound and infect it. It also helps hold the wound together as it heals.

▷ Medicine can be taken to kill germs or correct problems inside the body. Some medicines are swallowed, but others are injected through the skin.

◁ Problems inside the body can require surgery in an operating room. The surgeon makes an opening in the body, repairs the problem, and then sews it up again. Here, a surgeon opens a person's skull to operate on the brain, while other doctors look at a scan of the problem area.

Find Out More

Our bodies
10–11

Infection
62–63

Spare parts

More and more these days, artificial parts are used to repair the body if something goes wrong. These parts include artificial limbs, false teeth, pacemakers, and metal joints. Some scientists are trying to develop robots that will one day be able to behave exactly the same way as humans.

◁ This robot has a shape that looks human, but it cannot copy all human activities because it does not have human intelligence.

△ This Afghan boy had part of his right leg blown off when he stepped on a land mine. He has been fitted with an artificial leg and is now trying to return to a normal life at a rehabilitation (recovery) center.

▷ This girl does not have any artificial body parts. If she did need them, the body parts shown are all available today. By the time she is grown up, many more parts will have been developed to replace worn out or damaged areas of the body.

▷ Computers are becoming more complex all the time, but no computer is as intelligent as a human brain.

▷ A metal plate is screwed over a skull fracture to protect it as it heals.

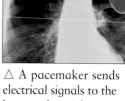

◁ Sometimes an artificial eye is used to replace a damaged or diseased eye.

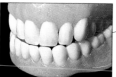

△ False teeth, or dentures, are used by patients whose teeth have been removed or have fallen out.

△ A pacemaker sends electrical signals to the heart to keep it beating at a regular rate.

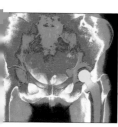

△ This X ray shows a metal hip joint. The diseased joint is replaced to help the patient walk properly.

▷ An artificial leg is used when a person's leg has been amputated. The leg has a cup into which the stump of the leg fits, and joints at the knee and ankle to make it flexible.

△ This man has an artificial forearm. Signals from the muscles in the upper arm allow the hand to move and grip.

Find Out More

Bones and joints
24–25

Control center
34–35

Amazing facts

Everything about the human body is incredible. There are hundreds of amazing facts and records about everything in your body, from your smallest cells to your largest organs. You will have read about many of these in this book, but here are a few more really astounding facts.

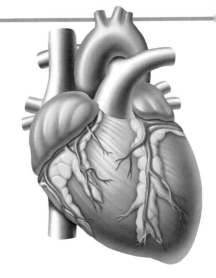

Blueprint for life
• Most of the body's 50 trillion cells contain 46 sets of instructions, called chromosomes, that run the cell and build a human body.
• Individual instructions in the chromosome are called genes. There are over 100,000 genes in each cell.

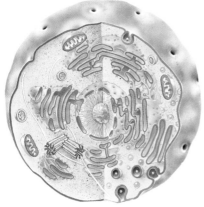

Shelf life
• Some cells live for a matter of days, while others last for years. In most cases, old cells are replaced instantly.
• Cells lining the small intestine survive for three to six days before being worn away.

• Cells in the epidermis of the skin live for about 25 days before flaking off. About 36 million are shed every day.
• Red blood cells live for about 120 days.
• Liver cells live for about 500 days.
• Bone cells live for many years.
• Many nerve cells survive for a lifetime, although the brain loses about 1,000 cells eac day which are not replaced. (Don't worry, thi doesn't make you any less intelligent!)

Mass production
• Some types of body cells are produced in huge numbers every day.
• To carry oxygen around the body, 170 billion red blood cells are produced daily
• To fight disease, 10 billion white blood cells are produced daily.
• In a man's testes, 300 million sperm are produced every day.

Gut facts
• If you stretched out the digestive system in a straight line, it would be more than three times the height of an adult.
• The longest part of the digestive system is the small intestine, which is about 17 feet long—longer than most cars.

Nail facts
• Fingernails grow about $^1/_5$ inch each month.
• Your fingernails grow four times faster than your toenails.
• Both fingernails and toenails grow faster in the summer than in the winter.
• The fingernails on your dominant hand (depending on whether you are right-handed or left-handed) grow slightly faster than the fingernails on the other hand.

Nervous information
• Nerve cells, or neurons, are the longest cells in the body and can be up to three feet in length.
• Electrical nerve impulses can travel along neurons at up to 250 miles per hour.
• Laid end to end, the nerves in your body would stretch for an incredible 47 miles!

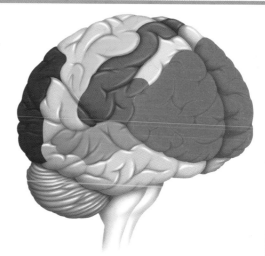

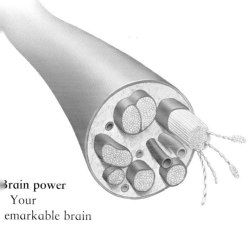

Brain power
Your remarkable brain contains over 100 billion nerve cells.
Keeping your brain working needs a colossal amount of oxygen and glucose to give it energy.
Although the brain weighs just 2 percent of your body weight, it uses 20 percent of your body's oxygen, 20 percent of its fuel supply, and 15 percent of its blood.

Gas exchanges
• Every day you breathe in and out about 25,000 times, with about 3,250 gallons of air traveling through your lungs.
• Everyone releases up to two quarts of gas, called flatus, through their anus every day—enough to fill a balloon.

Hairy stories
• Your hair grows about half an inch every month.
• If hair is not cut, it usually stops growing when it gets about 24 inches long.
• Some women can grow their hair very long indeed. The record length was nearly 13 feet!

Life records
• The average height of adult women is 5 feet, 5 inches, and 5 feet, 9$^1/_2$ inches for adult men. In some parts of the world, children are growing to be much taller than their parents, because they have a better, more nutritious diet when they are young.
• In a normal lifetime, an average person eats 33 tons of food, produces 9,300 gallons of urine, and has 319,200,000 pints of blood pumped around their body!

Body quiz

How much do you know about the human body? Try these questions to test your knowledge. The answers can all be found somewhere in the book (and on page 103).

(and on page 103).

TRUE OR FALSE?

1. Watching TV is better exercise than walking.

True or False?

2. The left side of your brain controls the right side of your body.

True or False?

3. Sweating helps keep your body warm.

True or False?

4. Identical twins have identical fingerprints.

True or False?

5. Neuron is another name for a nerve cell.

True or False?

6. You only produce tears when you are crying.

True or False?

7. Reflex actions, like blinking, happen without you thinking about them.

True or False?

8. You have millions of harmless germs inside your body.

True or False?

9. White blood cells carry oxygen around the body.

True or False?

10. Arteries are blood vessels that carry blood toward the heart.

True or False?

11. Your sense of taste is 10,000 times more sensitive than your sense of smell.

True or False?

12. Light is detected in the eyes by sensors called rods and cones.

True or False?

13. Babies can walk when they are six months old.

True or False?

14. Chicken and fish are two foods that are rich in fiber.

True or False?

15. You have an anvil, a stirrup, and a hammer in your body.

True or False?

16. Water makes up about one fourth of your body's weight.

True or False?

WHICH ANSWER CORRECTLY COMPLETES EACH STATEMENT?

1. The clear part at the front of your eye is called the:

a) carina
b) corona
c) cornea

2. Your lungs are spongy because they are filled with millions of tiny air bags called:

a) alveoli
b) ravioli
c) aioli

3. Your heart beats to pump blood around the body:

a) all the time, at the same rate whatever you are doing
b) all the time, but speeds up when you exercise
c) during the day, but stops at night for a rest

4. Just over half of your balanced diet should be made up of:

a) starchy foods such as rice, potatoes, bread, or pasta
b) protein foods such as poultry, fish, eggs, and beans
c) fatty foods such as dairy products, burgers, and french fries

5. The waste liquid called urine that comes out of your body when you go to the bathroom is made in the:

a) stomach
b) kidneys
c) bladder

6. The brown pigment that colors your skin and protects it from sunlight is called:

a) melanin
b) melanie
c) melamine

7. You lose skin flakes from the surface of your skin all the time as your clothes rub against it. Each year you lose a total of:

a) nine ounces of skin flakes
b) nine pounds of skin flakes
c) nine tons of skin flakes

8. The longest part of your digestive system is the:

a) large intestine
b) esophagus
c) small intestine

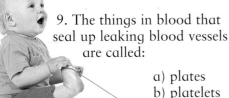

9. The things in blood that seal up leaking blood vessels are called:

a) plates
b) platelets
c) platters

10. The packages of instructions found inside each cell that control all your body's features are called:

a) chromospheres
b) chromosomes
c) chronometers

11. The normal temperature inside the body is about:

a) 212°F (boiling)
b) 120°F (hot)
c) 98.6°F (very warm)

12. The type of teeth that crush food in your mouth is called:

a) molars
b) incisors
c) canines

13. The best exercise for improving your stamina would be:

a) swimming
b) ballet
c) push-ups

14. In bright light, the pupils of your eyes get:

a) wider
b) narrower
c) stay the same

15. Your muscles are attached to your bones by tough cords called:

a) ligaments
b) cartilage
c) tendons

16. The air that you breathe out contains:

a) more oxygen than the air you breathe in
b) less oxygen than the air you breathe in
c) the same amount of oxygen as the air you breathe in

17. Your body needs a constant supply of glucose:

a) as a building material for growth and repair
b) to give your body the energy it needs
c) as a carrier to remove poisonous wastes

18. The chemicals that break down food during digestion are called:

a) enzymes
b) hormones
c) nutrients

19. The time in their early teens when boys and girls grow rapidly is called:

a) probity
b) publicly
c) puberty

ANSWERS

TRUE OR FALSE?

1. False. Walking is much better exercise than watching TV.

2. True. Each side of the body is controlled by the opposite side of the brain.

3. False. Sweating helps cool your body down.

4. False. Identical twins may be identical in most ways, but no two people have the same fingerprints—not even identical twins.

5. True. Neurons are very long cells that transmit electrical nerve messages all around the body.

6. False. You produce tears all the time to keep the front of your eyes clean and moist. You produce more tears when you cry.

7. True. The brain is only informed about the action after the muscles have moved.

8. True. Millions of germs called bacteria live inside your digestive system. Some of them help with digestion.

9. False. Red blood cells carry oxygen around the body.

10. False. Arteries are blood vessels that carry blood away from the heart.

11. False. Your sense of smell is 10,000 times more sensitive than your sense of taste.

12. True. Rods detect black and white, and cones detect colors.

13. False. Infants start to walk by themselves when they are about a year old.

14. False. Meat and fish do not contain fiber. Fruit and vegetables do.

15. True. These are names for the three tiny ossicle bones in your ear.

16. False. Water is about two thirds of your weight.

WHICH ANSWER CORRECTLY COMPLETES EACH STATEMENT?

1. c) cornea

2. a) alveoli

3. b) all the time, but speeds up when you exercise

4. a) starchy foods such as rice, potatoes, bread, or pasta

5. b) kidneys

6. a) melanin

7. b) nine pounds of skin flakes

8. c) small intestine. It is about 17 feet long.

9. b) platelets

10. b) chromosomes

11. c) 98.6°F (very warm)

12. a) molars

13. a) swimming

14. b) narrower

15. c) tendons

16. b) less oxygen than the air you breathe in

17. b) to give your body the energy it needs

18. a) enzymes

19. c) puberty

Glossary

A glossary is like a mini-dictionary. It explains some of the hard words in the main part of the book. If you come across a word you do not know, you will probably find it listed here. Next to the word, you will find an explanation of what it means. Like a dictionary, the glossary is arranged in alphabetical order.

abdomen The lower part of the main body between your chest and your legs. The abdomen contains your stomach and other organs involved in digesting food, as well as your two kidneys and bladder.

alveoli The millions of tiny air bags found in your lungs. Oxygen passes from the air into your bloodstream through alveoli.

anesthetic A special medicine that makes you sleep very deeply, so that a doctor can operate on you.

atrium The left atrium and right atrium are chambers in the upper part of the heart. The plural of atrium is "atria."

balanced diet Your diet is what you eat. A balanced diet is one that gives your body a wide range of nutrients—fats, proteins, carbohydrates, vitamins, and minerals— in the right amounts needed for good health.

blood vessel A tube that carries blood through the body. The main types of blood vessels are arteries, veins, and capillaries.

cancer A disease caused by cells dividing out of control. When they do this, they produce growths called tumors that keep the body from working correctly. There are a lot of different types of cancers, many of which can be treated by doctors.

carbohydrates These are nutrients that supply your body with energy. Foods rich in carbohydrates include pasta, potatoes, and rice.

carbon dioxide A type of gas found in the air around you. When your cells release energy from food, they release carbon dioxide as waste. This is carried to the lungs and breathed out into the air.

cartilage A tough, rubbery material that supports parts of your body such as your nose and ears. It also covers the ends of bones where they meet in joints.

cells Your body is made up of billions of these tiny, living units. There are many different types of cells, each with a different job to do.

cerebrum The main part of your brain. The wrinkled cerebrum allows you to feel, think, speak, and see, and it makes your body move.

chromosome X-shaped packages of information found inside every one of your body's cells. Chromosomes contain the instructions needed to build a living human being.

cochlea A part of the inner ear that is shaped like a snail's shell. The cochlea picks up sound waves and sends messages to the brain so that you can hear.

cranium The upper, dome-shaped part of the skull that surrounds the brain and keeps it from being damaged.

diabetes A disease caused by the lack of a hormone called insulin, which is produced by the pancreas. Insulin makes sure there is enough glucose in your blood to give you energy. People with diabetes need to inject themselves with insulin to keep glucose levels normal.

diaphragm A sheet of muscle that separates your chest from your abdomen. Your diaphragm plays an important part in breathing.

digestion The process by which the food you eat is broken down into simple nutrients that your body can use. Digestion takes place inside the digestive system.

enzyme A special substance that helps to break food down into simple nutrients during digestion.

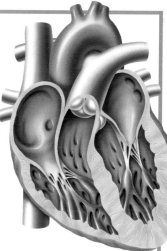

fats These are nutrients that are used to give you energy, and to help build your body. Fats are stored under the skin, to keep you warm. Foods rich in fats include milk and other dairy products, meat, and eggs.

fertilization The joining together of an egg from a woman and a sperm from a man. A fertilized egg produced by fertilization grows and develops into a baby.

fiber Material found in plant foods such as fruits and beans. Although fiber is not digested, it is important because it makes digestion work efficiently.

fetus The name given to the baby developing inside the mother's uterus from eight weeks after fertilization until it is born.

hormones Chemical messengers produced by special glands such as the pituitary gland and the pancreas. Hormones are carried by the blood to tell parts of your body what to do.

joint Part of the skeleton where two or more bones meet. Some joints, like those in the skull, are fixed. Most are flexible and allow the body to move.

melanin The brown pigment (coloring) found in skin that gives it its color and protects it from the harmful effects of sunlight. Melanin also gives hair its color.

minerals This is a group of nutrients needed in small amounts to make sure your body works correctly. Foods rich in minerals include fresh fruit and vegetables, cereals, nuts, fish and seafood, dairy products, and meat.

muscle A part of the body that can contract (get shorter). Over 640 skeletal muscles (muscles attached to your bones) are controlled by your brain to pull the bones and make your body move.

nephrons Tiny filtering units found inside your kidneys. Nephrons clean your blood by removing poisonous waste and excess water to make urine.

neurons Nerve cells that make up your nervous system and carry electrical messages at high speed. Neurons have a thin, very long section called a nerve fiber that carries messages between your brain and all parts of your body. Nerve fibers are bundled together.

nucleus The control center of every body cell. The nucleus contains 46 chromosomes that carry the instructions needed to build and operate that cell.

nutrients Substances contained in the food you eat that are needed to keep you alive. Nutrients supply your body with energy and the raw materials needed for growth and repair.

organ A major part of the body such as the brain, kidney, or heart. Each organ does a specific job.

oxygen A type of gas found in the air. Oxygen is essential for life. You take it in through your lungs. Your cells use oxygen to release energy from food.

papillae The little bumps found on the surface of your tongue. Papillae contain taste buds, which detect tastes in food and drinks.

plaque A deposit of bacteria and food that builds up on teeth if they are not cleaned well. Bacteria in plaque releases substances that cause tooth decay.

proteins These are nutrients used by your body for growth and repair. Foods rich in proteins include fish, chicken, meat, and beans.

reflex An automatic action such as blinking, swallowing, or pulling your hand away from a hot object, which you do without thinking about it.

skeleton The framework of 206 bones that supports your body, allows you to move, and protects delicate organs such as the brain.

suture The joints between skull bones that do not allow movement. In a suture, the bones are locked together like pieces in a jigsaw puzzle.

sweat A salty, waste liquid produced by the skin, especially when you are hot. When sweat evaporates (goes into the air) from your skin's surface, it draws heat from your body and cools you down.

system A group of organs that work together to do a particular job. The esophagus, stomach, and intestines, for example, make up the digestive system, which digests your food.

tendon A tough cord that connects the end of a muscle to a bone. When the muscle contracts, it pulls the bone using the tendon.

tissue A collection of cells of the same type that work together. Different tissues form an organ.

umbilical cord The cord containing blood vessels that links a fetus to the mother when it is inside her uterus. The umbilical cord carries food and oxygen to the fetus and removes the waste.

urine The liquid waste made in the kidneys. Urine is stored in the bladder, which is emptied when you go to the bathroom.

vaccine A medicine given to a person, often by injection, that helps protect them against particular diseases.

ventricle One of the two lower chambers—right and left—of the heart. The right ventricle pumps blood to the lungs; the left pumps blood to the rest of the body.

villi Tiny fingerlike projections that line the inside of your small intestine. Villi make sure that, after digestion, nutrients go into your bloodstream as quickly as possible.

vitamins This is a group of nutrients needed in small amounts by your body to make sure it works correctly. Foods rich in vitamins include fresh fruit and vegetables, cereals, eggs, fish, and meat.

Index

This index helps you find subjects in this book. It is in alphabetical order. Main entries are in dark, or bold, type.

E

ear canals 46, 47
eardrums 47
ears 20, 21, **46–47**
eating **70–71**, 73, 74–75, 82, 91, 99
eggs **78–79**, 80, 86, 87
elbows 10
enamel 73
endocrine glands 54, 55
energy 13, **70–71**, 90–91, 92, 93, 99
enzymes 70, 74
epidermis 14, 15, 16, 50–51, 98
epiglottis 73
esophagus 73, 74–75
excitement 54
exercise 26–27, 90–91
expressions 10, 28–29
eye sockets 22, 23, 43
eyebrows 28, 29
eyelashes 44
eyelids 29, 44
eyes **42–45**, 68, 86, 97

F

face 10, 22–23, **28–29**
fallopian tubes 78, 79
false teeth 96
family tree **86–87**
farsightedness 44
fat (body) 15, 16
fats (food) 91, 92–93
fear 54
feces 75
feelings 15, 28–29, 32, 34, 52–53, 54, **88–89**
feet 10
females 11, 55, 78–79, 80–81, 99

fetus 80–81
fever 62
fiber (food) 92–93
fibers (body) 12, 27, 30, 33
filaments 47
fingernails 99
fingerprints 14, 31
fingers **30–31**, 44, 50, 51
flatus 99
flexibility 90
follicles (egg) 79
follicles (hair) 14, 15, 18, 19
food 48, 72, 73, **92–93**
forehead 27, 29
freckles 17
frowning 28, 29
fruit 92–93

G

gas 99
genes 98
germs 14, 60, 61, **62–63**, 75, 94, 95
glucose 55, 99
good health 90–93
goosebumps 15
gripping 31
growing 23, 54, 71, **84–85**, 92, 99
gums 72, 73

H

hair 14, **18–19**, 54, 99
hair color 19, 85
hair follicles 14, 15, 18, 19
hammer 21
hands **30–31**, 50
hay fever 68
head **22–23**, 25, 58, 59, 83, 84

hearing 21, 34, 35, 38, **46–47**, 52
heart 29, **56–57**, 58, 59, 97
heartbeats 56, 57, 59
heart rate 35, 54
heart valves 56, 57
height 99
hinge joints 24
hips 20, 21, 97
hormones **54–55**
hunger 70, 83

I

incisors 72
incubators 82
infection **62–63**, 95
insulin 55
intelligence 97
iris 42, 43, 45
itch mites 15

J

jawbone **22–23**, 72
joints **24–25**, 90, 96, 97

K

kidneys 76–77
kneecap 20
knees 24, 25, 27, 37, 97

L

large intestine 74–75, 98
larynx 52, 53
learning **38–39**, 82–83, 84
left-handedness 35, 98–99
legs 21, 37, 91, 96

The publisher would like to thank the following for contributing to this book:

Photographs

b = bottom, c = center, l = left, r = right, t = top

Page 12 *tr* Pr S.Cinti/CNRI/SPL, *c* CNRI/SPL, *cl* Pr P.M. Motta & T. Fujita/University "La Sapienza," Rome/SPL, *bc* Pr P.M. Motta & S.Correr/SPL; 13 *bc* SPL; 14 *cl* Martin Dohrn/SPL, *c* Quest/SPL; 15 *tc* Martin Dohrn/SPL, *cr* Richard Wehr/Custom Medical Stock Photo/SPL, *br* SPL; 16–17 Telegraph Colour Library/Mel Yates; 17 *bc* SPL; 18 *cl* Telegraph Colour Library/Michael Krasowitz, *c* Images Colour Library; 18–19 David Scharf/SPL; 20 *cl* Scott Camazine/SPL; *cr* CNRI/SPL; 21 *cr* James Stevenson/SPL, 25 *cr* Pr P. Motta/Dept. of Anatomy/University "La Sapienza," Rome/SPL, *bl* CNRI/SPL; 27 *tr* Biophoto Associates/SPL, *cr* Robbie Jack; 29 *c* Adam Hart-Davis/SPL, *cr* Adam Hart-Davis/SPL, 30 *cl* John Birdsall Photography/Clare Marsh, *br* Martin Dohrn/SPL; 35 *cr* GJLP/SPL, *c* CNRI/SPL; 37 *tl* Liysa King/Image Bank, *cr* Taeke Henstra/Petit Format, *bl* Pascal Brousse/Petit Format; 38 *cl* Wellcome Dept. of Cognitive Neurology/SPL, *tr* Montreal Neuro Institute/McGill University/CNRI/SPL; 38–39 John Warmsley; 39 *bl* Bubbles Photo Library/LoisJoy Thurston; *cr* Tony Stone Images/David Young Wolff; 40 *tl* Hank Morgan/SPL, *tc* Hank Morgan/SPl, *cr* John Greim/SPL, *bc* Will & Deni McIntyre/SPL; 42 *tr* Adam Hart-Davis/SPL, *cr* Adam Hart-Davis/SPL; 43 *tr* Omikron/SPL; 44 *cr* Tony Stone Images/Terry Vine; 47 *tl* Wellcome Trust Medical Photographic Library, *tc* Pr P. Motta/Dept. of Anatomy/University "La Sapienza," Rome, SPL; 49 *cr* Omikron/SPL, *br* (papillae) Prof P. Motta/Dept. of Anatomy/University "La Sapienza," Rome/SPL; 52 *cl* Tony Stone Images/Mary Kate Denny; 54 *bl* Tony Stone Images/Laurence Monneret; 54–55 Tony Stone Images/Doug Armand; 55 *cr* Chris Priest & Mark Clarke/SPL; 56 *cl* SPL; 57 *tl* Tony Stone Iamges/Charles Thatcher, *bl* SPL; 59 *tl* CNRI/SPL, *cr* CNRI/SPL; 60 *c* Damien Lovergrove/SPL, *bl* BSIP, LBL/SPL; 61 Wellcome Trust Medical Photographic Library, 62 *cl* David Scharf/SPL, *br* Petit Format/Malvina Mendil; 62–63 Biology Media/SPL, 64 *cl* Tony Stone Images/Chris Harvey; 65 *cr* J.C. Revy/SPL; 67 *cr* Eddy Gray/SPl, *bc* Collections/Dorothy Burrows; 68 *cl* Damien Lovegrove/SPL, *bc* David Scharf/SPL; 68–69 Matt Meadows, Peter Arnold Inc/SPL; 69 *tl* Yoram Lehmann/Still Pictures, *tr* Matt Meadows, Peter Arnold Inc./SPL, *cr* H.Schleichkorn/Custom Medical Stock Photo/SPL; 71 *cr* Petit Format/J.P. Vidal; 73 *bl* CNRI/SPL; 74 *cl* Dr Klaus Schiller/SPL; 75 *tc* Eye of Science/SPL;

79 *bc* Motta & Familiari/Anatomy Dept./University "La Sapienza," Rome/SPL, *cr* Prof. P.M. Motta G. Macchiarelli, SA Nottola/SPL; 80 *bc* Wellcome Trust Medical Photographic Library; 81 *c* PH Saada/Eurelios/SPL, *cr* Images Photo Library, *bc* Petit Format/Nestle/SPL; 82 *br* Peter Ryan/SPL; 83 Bubbles/Susanna Price; 84 *cl* Images Colour Library, *c* BSIP Boucharlat/SPL, *bl* Petit Format/Agnes Chaumat; 85 *cr* Images Colour Library, *bc* Images Colour Library, *c* Panos Pictures/Sean Sprague; 86 Biophoto Associates/SPL; 88 *bc* Lawrence Migdale/SPL; 88–89 Mark Edwards/Still Pictures; 89 *tl* Panos Pictures/Mark McEvoy, *tr* Images Colour Library, *cr* Panos Pictures/Sean Sprague, *bl* Panos Pictures/Penny Tweedie; 90 *cl* Tony Stone Images/Frank Siteman, *bl* Tony Stone Images/David Madison; 91 *bl* Tony Stone Images/Donna Day, *cr* Tony Stone Iamges/David Young Wolff; 92–93 Tony Stone Images/John Kelly; 93 *tl* Tony Stone Images/Carin Krasner, *cr* Tony Stone Images/Sara Taylor; 94 *cl* Tony Stone Images/Julian Calder, *bl* Wellcome Trust Medical Photographic Library; 94–95 Tony Stone Images/Mark Harme; 95 *tr* Dept. of Clinical Radiology, Salisbury District Hospital/SPL, *cr* BSIP Laurent/Science Photo Library; 96 *tr* Panos Pictures/Heldur Netocny/Pakistan, *cl* US Department of Energy/SPL, *b* Tony Stone Images/Mary Kate Denny; 97 *tl (teeth)* Science Pictures Ltd/SPL, *tl* James Stevenson/SPL, *tr* James Stevenson/SPL; *cr* Dept. of Clinical Radiology, Salisbury District Hospital/SPL, *cl* Mehau Kulyk/SPL, *bl* Wellcome Trust Medical Photographic Library, *br* Peter Menzel/SPL.

Every effort has been made to trace the copyright holders of the photographs. The publishers apologize for any inconvenience caused.

Additional illustrations

Mike Atkinson, Peter Bull, Robin Carter, Ruth Lindsay, Jonathan Potter, Mike Saunders, Rob Shone, Linda Thursby, Ray Turvey.

Models

Ajay Athwal, Bibbanpreet Bahd, Rajpriya Bahd, Molly Bray, Cristóbal Castillo, Brian Cusack, Christopher Davis, Eleanor Davis, Mike Davis, Teresa Davis, Marianne Gingell, Trey Horne, Lucy Jennings, James McMeeken, Jake Marley, Sanjeevan Paramothayan, Gabriel Porter-Tierney, Angelina Sidonio, Dominic Sidonio, Philippa Stroud, William Swart, Alice Wright.